SISTER PEG

Cambridge Studies in the History and Theory of Politics

EDITORS

Maurice Cowling, G. R. Elton,
E. Kedourie, J. R. Pole,
Walter Ullmann

SISTER PEG

A pamphlet hitherto unknown
by David Hume

edited with an introduction
and notes by

DAVID R. RAYNOR

CAMBRIDGE UNIVERSITY PRESS

CAMBRIDGE

LONDON   NEW YORK   NEW ROCHELLE

MELBOURNE   SYDNEY

Published by the Press Syndicate of the University of Cambridge
The Pitt Building, Trumpington Street, Cambridge CB2 1RP
32 East 57th Street, New York, NY 10022, USA
296 Beaconsfield Parade, Middle Park, Melbourne 3206, Australia

First published 1982

Printed in Great Britain at
Western Printing Services Ltd, Bristol

Library of Congress catalogue card number: 81–18042

British Library Cataloguing in Publication Data

Hume, David
Sister Peg. – (Cambridge studies in the history
and theory of politics)
1. Great Britain – Politics and government –
18th century – Anecdotes, facetiae, satire, etc.
I. Title   II. Raynor, David
828'.608   PR3687.S4

ISBN 0 521 24299 1

CONTENTS

v

ACKNOWLEDGEMENTS

I am much indebted to Lord Dacre of Glanton, David Kettler, and Quentin Skinner, for their valuable comments on an earlier draft of the introduction. Most of their suggestions have been incorporated into my final draft. The usual disclaimer that they are not responsible for the result is especially appropriate in a work of this kind, where I have had to rely entirely upon probability, and could not 'call up the Devil by any powerful Incantation and oblige him to speak Truth'.

DAVID R. RAYNOR

INTRODUCTION

The first volume of Hume's *History of England*, on the reigns of James I and Charles I, was published in 1754, followed three years later by a volume on the Commonwealth and the reigns of Charles II and James II. Thereafter Hume wrote his history backwards – as witches say their prayers. After the Tudor volumes were published in March 1759, Hume paused in order to decide how to continue his narrative. Many people urged him to write the reigns of King William and Queen Anne. 'This work', he confessed, 'would be more entertaining both to me & the public, than the diving into old, barbarous & obscure Reigns; where I could scarce hope to communicate any thing new, and might even fail of making my Narration entertaining.'[1] But Hume eventually decided to continue to work backwards, and in July 1759 began writing the history of England from the invasion of Julius Caesar to the accession of the house of Tudor.[2] Several months later he informed his publisher that 'this Part of English History is a Work of infinite Labour & Study; which however I do not grudge: For I have nothing better nor more agreeable to employ me'.[3] But it appears that during the summer of 1760 Hume also entertained himself by composing a sustained political satire.

In *The Life of David Hume* Ernest C. Mossner revealed that in 1761 Hume wrote a political satire directed against William Pitt. This publication is mentioned in a letter from Rear-Admiral George Murray to his brother, General James Murray, Governor of Quebec:

David Hume values him selfe on prognosticating your greatness. I wanted him to write to you but he thought it might appear for ward, tho I assur'd him had you conquerd the old world as well as the new his correspondence woud a been acceptable. He has wrote a houmorous

I

thing I here by send you which has done no good to your friend. Still as he is exprest by no name but Gowler . . .[4]

Mossner concluded that it would probably not be worth searching for this publication; however, I shall argue that we do not need to search for it in the pamphlet literature of 1761, for there is reason to believe that this hitherto unlocated publication is *The History of the Proceedings in the Case of Margaret, Commonly called Peg, only lawful Sister to John Bull, Esq.*; a work which is usually ascribed to Adam Ferguson, primarily on the basis of the testimony of the Reverend Alexander Carlyle of Inveresk.

It would not have been Hume's first political satire. In 1748 he published *A True Account of the Behaviour and Conduct of Archibald Stewart, Esq.; late Lord Provost of Edinburgh*; a witty fifty-one page defence of his friend, who was on trial for having surrendered Edinburgh without a fight to the Jacobite forces during the Rebellion of 1745. Hume never publicly acknowledged authorship of this pamphlet because 'the Subject was rather too particular, as well as for other Reasons'.[5] In 1750 and 1751 Hume wrote skits against James Fraser, a Jacobite acquaintance.[6] And in 1751, when the Church of Scotland ministers petitioned parliament for a pay increase, Hume composed a short piece ridiculing their request, and circulated copies of the manuscript to intimate friends. To Dr Clephane he wrote: 'Since I am in the humour of displaying my wit, I must tell you that lately, at an idle hour, I wrote a sheet called the Bellman's Petition: wherein (if I be not partial, which I certainly am) there was some good pleasantry and satire.'[7] Hume revealed his intentions behind this skit to Gilbert Elliot:

I send you enclos'd a little Endeavour at Drollery against some People who care not much to be jok'd upon. I have frequently had it in my Intentions to write a Supplement to *Gulliver*, containing the Ridicule of Priests. Twas certainly a Pity that Swift was a Parson. Had he been a Lawyer or Physician, we had nevertheless been entertain'd at the Expense of these Professions. But Priests are so jealous, that they cannot bear to be touch'd on that Head; and for a plain Reason: Because they are conscious they are really ridiculous. That Part of the Doctor's Subject is so fertile, that a much inferior Genius, I am confident, might succeed in it.[8]

Since the Edinburgh printers refused to print this pamphlet,

Hume had it brought out in London under the pseudonym of Zerobabel MacGilchrist, Bellman of Buckhaven. Elliot reacted coldly towards it, and Hume himself later regretted that he had ever had it printed:

Not because it will give Offence, but because it will not give Entertainment: Not because it may be call'd profane; but because it may perhaps be deservedly call'd dull. To tell the Truth, I was always so indifferent about Fortune, & especially now, that I am more advanc'd in Life, & am a little more at my Ease, suited to my extreme Frugality, that I neither fear nor hope any thing from any man, and am very indifferent either about Offence or Favour. Not only, I woud not sacrifice Truth & Reason to political Views, but scarce even a Jest. You may tell me that I ought to have revers'd the Order of these Points, & have put the Jest first: As it is usual for People to be the fondest of their Performances on Subjects on which they are least made to excel. And that, consequently, I would give more to be thought a good Droll, than to have the Praises of Erudition, & Subtility, & Invention. – This malicious Insinuation, I will give no Answer to. . .[9]

Sister Peg was published just before Christmas 1760 – 'elegantly printed in small Octavo, Price Two Shillings and Six Pence sewed' – and five weeks later Hume acknowledged that he had written it. To Dr Carlyle he wrote:

I am inform'd, that you have receiv'd a Letter from London, by which you learn that the Manuscript of *Sister Peg* has been trac'd to the Printer's, and has been found to be in many Places interlind & corrected in my hand-writing. I cou'd have wish'd, that you had not published this Piece of Intelligence before you told me of it. The Truth is, after I had compos'd that trifling Performance, and thought I had made it as correct as I cou'd, I gave it to a sure hand to be transcribed, that, and in case any of the London Printers had known my hand, they might not be able to discover me: But as it lay by me some Weeks afterwards, I coud not forbear reviewing it; and not having my Amanuensis at hand, I was oblig'd in several Places to correct it myself, rather than allow it to go to the Press [with] Inaccuracies of which I was sensible. I little dream'd, that this small Want of Precaution [wou'd have] betray'd me so soon. But as you know, that I am very indifferent about Princes or Preside[nts, Minist]ers of the Gospel or Ministers of State, Kings or Keysars, and set at Defiance all Powers, hum[an and] infernal; I had no other Reason for concealing myself but in order to try the Taste of the

3

Public, whom, tho I also set in some degree at Defiance, I cannot sometimes forbear paying a little regard to. I find, that that frivolous Composition has been better receivd than I had any Reason to expect; and therefore cannot much complain of the Injury you have done me by revealing my Secret, and obliging me to acknowledge it more early than I intended. The only Reason of my writing to you is to know the Printer's Name who has so far broke his Engagements as to show the Manuscript: For the Bookseller assurd my Friend, to whom I entrusted it, that we might depend upon an absolute Secrecy.[10]

Carlyle rejected Hume's claim because he believed that Adam Ferguson had written *Sister Peg*. Hume's letter acknowledging authorship has been universally regarded ever since as designed merely to throw people off the track of the real author, or to tease Carlyle.[11] Carlyle's account of the events immediately following publication of *Sister Peg* seems plausible; however, when examined carefully, its initial plausibility vanishes, and a very different explanation suggests itself.

After the defeat of the Scottish Militia Bill in April 1760, Carlyle claimed that he had been approached by an unidentified friend to write a satirical pamphlet against the two Scottish Members of Parliament who had opposed it. Carlyle himself had already written three successful political pamphlets, including an ironical pro-Pitt pamphlet and one favouring a Scottish militia.[12] However, since he was too busy to undertake this project, he suggested that Ferguson be asked to do it. Although his friend objected that Ferguson 'was excellent at Serious Works, but could turn Nothing into Ridicule, as he had no Humour', Carlyle believed that Ferguson had secretly undertaken and executed this work. Hence, when *Sister Peg* was published in late December 1760, Carlyle had no doubts as to its author. But Hume, being 'a great Blab', was excluded from the 'secret', and his boundless 'Curiosity and Credulity' led to 'a very Ludicrous scene' between him and his friend Dr John Jardine. Hume accused Jardine of being the author, and when Jardine protested that he was incapable of executing such a work, Hume guessed that Carlyle had written it, 'never Dreaming of Ferguson'. After Jardine refused to reveal the 'secret', Hume 'told him that he had written it himself in an Idle Hour, and Desir'd Jardine to Mention him as the Author everywhere, that it might not fall on some of us who were not so able to Bear it'. Carlyle himself confessed that he 'could not have believ'd' this episode 'had not David himself wrote me a Letter to that Purpose...'[13]

Carlyle composed his memoirs forty years after the events just described had occurred. But, even if they occurred more or less as he described them, he may have misinterpreted them. Hume may have accused Jardine of being the author of *Sister Peg*. But at least two interpretations of this behaviour are possible: either Hume earnestly believed that his friend was the real author, or he was simply teasing him. One who, like Carlyle, believed that Ferguson had written it, and that Hume had been kept out of the secret, would choose the former interpretation. But if we consider the personal relations between Hume and Jardine, the latter interpretation seems the most probable. Jardine was a busy man of affairs who published nothing except a few reviews in the first *Edinburgh Review*. Hume was often the butt of his jokes, and just as often reciprocated.[14] When Hume was being lionized in Paris he confided to Ferguson that he often wished for 'the sharpness of Dr Jardine, to correct and qualify so much lusciousness'.[15] Nor is it likely that Hume would have believed that Carlyle had written *Sister Peg*. For Carlyle had only recently written a very successful panegyric on Pitt, praising him for his patriotism, industry, eloquence, scholarship, and honesty. Yet in *Sister Peg* Pitt ('Jowler') is portrayed as a self-serving politician whose every move is subservient to 'getting fixed in the management of the business'.

What does ring true in Carlyle's narrative is the report that Hume never suspected Ferguson of having written it. If Carlyle is to be believed, nearly everyone in Edinburgh thought that he himself had written it. And, indeed, apart from the pro-Pitt pamphlet, Carlyle might have seemed a very reasonable guess. Hume suggested in his essay on miracles that, when someone tells of an improbable event, his testimony should be believed only if it is more improbable that he is a deceiver or has been deceived than that the event really happened. In the present case, it will be argued that it is more probable that Carlyle himself was deceived in thinking that he knew who the author was than that Ferguson was the author.

Not all of Ferguson's contemporaries believed that he possessed the capacity to produce a work as humorous and as elegant as *Sister Peg*. John Ramsay of Ochtertyre also identified Ferguson as the author, but added that 'it was supposed he got many hints from Lord Elibank and his set'.[16] There are indeed many reasons why Ferguson's contemporaries would not have singled him out as the author. Ferguson by most accounts was inclined to be serious rather than humorous. How could somebody with so little humour produce a witty Scriblerian piece? The author of *Sister Peg* obviously had an excellent command of style; but Ferguson's works exhibited a poor style.[17] Ferguson himself admitted that his *Reflections Previous to the Establishment of a Militia* was 'a tedious Performance'.[18] And Hume thought that Ferguson's *Essay on the History of Civil Society* was not 'fit to be given to the Public, neither on account of the Style nor the Reasoning'.[19] In short, Ferguson never adequately mastered the English language, let alone the idiom of Grub Street. His remarks on militias in the *Essay* and *Reflections* seldom rise above exhortation, whereas the author of *Sister Peg* marshalls good arguments against bad arguments. Ferguson was a Highlander and a Gaelic speaker; it is unlikely that he would have described his fellow Highlanders as 'curious fellows' and have given them the generic name of 'MacLurchar', with its pejorative connotations of erratic staggering gait and sneak thievery. Moreover, with the possible exception of *Sister Peg*, Ferguson, as far as we know, never composed any satirical works. It therefore seems unreasonable to assume that he had the capacity to write a sustained political satire in the manner of Arbuthnot's *History of John Bull*.

But, if Ferguson did not write *Sister Peg*, why did he not deny authorship? If Hume had written it, why did he ever acknowledge authorship, and why did he do so when he did? And how could the Reverend Alexander Carlyle have been permanently deceived about the matter?

Carlyle had an inflated opinion of Ferguson ('if Reid is the Aristotle, Ferguson is the Plato of Scotch philosophers'), and comes across in his memoirs as a self-important braggart and gossip. There is reason to believe that Hume did not think highly of Carlyle.[20] If so, then Carlyle himself may have been kept out of the secret as to the author of the satire. Why, then, would Hume have revealed his secret to Carlyle? Two hypotheses seem plausible: Hume's letter may have been occasioned either by a

joke at his expense, or by a desire to protect his friends. If, as
Carlyle relates, Hume had been excluded from the secret, he
probably would have been disinclined to deceive the public in
order to protect the supposed but unknown clerical author(s).
But if Hume himself had written it, and if he believed that as a
result his clerical friends were suffering, then the honourable
course would have been to divert the bigots from his innocent
friends by acknowledging his authorship. Scotland 'is the Seat
of my principal friendships', he once told Adam Smith, 'but it
is too narrow for me, and it mortifies me that I sometimes hurt
my friends'.[21] On the other hand, if Hume had written *Sister
Peg*, and Jardine or Ferguson in jest had told him that the manuscript had been traced to the printers and had been found to bear
his handwriting, then Hume undoubtedly would have been
offended by the breach of trust, and would have attempted to
discover the culprit who had shown the manuscript. A decade
later, when 'some rascally Bookseller' intended to print Hume's
suppressed essays, Hume suspected 'some Infidelity or Negli-
gence' and sought to 'learn from what hand he had the copy'.[22]
On either hypothesis we can construct an account of the events
surrounding the publication of *Sister Peg* which is consistent
with all of the presently available evidence and with the honour
of Hume, Ferguson, and Carlyle. Let us suppose that in August
Ferguson accepts the commission to write the satire, and brings
Hume in as a collaborator. But Ferguson is busy preparing his
lectures in natural philosophy (a subject he knows little about)
so that the project falls to Hume alone. When *Sister Peg* is published, Carlyle lets a dozen people into the 'secret' that Ferguson
is the author. Hume has carefully concealed his authorship in
order to try the taste of the public, and Ferguson has promised
not to reveal the secret. The rumour that Ferguson is the author
furthers his interest with his patrons, Lord Milton and Lord
Bute. But Hume's abundantly prudent clerical friends believe
that the satire will hurt the moderate cause. After teasing Jardine,
Hume reveals his secret. In return, Jardine tells Hume that the
secret is already out, because Carlyle has traced the manuscript
to the printers and discovered that Hume is the real author.
Hume writes to Carlyle in order to find out 'the Printer's Name
who has so far broke his Engagements as to show the Manuscript. . . .'.

7

We have seen that it is unlikely that Ferguson wrote *Sister Peg*, and that Carlyle's narrative and Hume's letter to Carlyle can be accounted for without assuming that Ferguson wrote the satire. But is it plausible that Hume wrote a sequel to Arbuthnot's *History of John Bull*?

Hume, unlike Ferguson, identified with the Tory wits of Queen Anne's time. In 1734 he wrote a long autobiographical letter to Dr Arbuthnot.[23] Several years later he presented a copy of *A Treatise of Human Nature* to Alexander Pope. And in middle life Hume reported, with obvious satisfaction, that he was visiting 'at a kind of classical Place, celebrated by Pope, Swift &c [a]nd with a classical Man, who livd in Intimacy with these two wits and with Prior, Gay, Arbuthnot, Bolingbroke & every Person celebrated in his time'.[24] J. G. A. Pocock has observed that by the 1770s, with the expansion of empire and the vast increase in the public debt, Hume's splenetic pronouncements in private correspondence place him squarely in 'the tradition of Swift and Bolingbroke, denouncing Pitt, as they had once denounced Marlborough, as the author of war, debt and corruption'.[25] It therefore appears plausible that Hume's ambition to write a supplement to *Gulliver's Travels* was accompanied by a similar ambition to write a sequel to the *History of John Bull*.

Hume's strong pronouncements against mercenary armies, and in favour of citizen militias, have led a recent writer to remark that it is surprising that Hume's *Essays Moral and Political* did not include an essay on this controversial political issue.[26] After all, Hume concluded the first Stuart volume of his *History* by remarking that the events of the Civil War furnish us with a useful lesson 'concerning the madness of the people, the furies of fanaticism, and the danger of mercenary armies'.[27] But his concern with this issue is evident even in the political essays of the 1740s. When he wrote in 1741 that public liberty had declined during Walpole's administration he was asked to give instances supporting this charge. 'There are many instances', he replied, 'tho', I hope, none fatal; such as, the increase of the civil list, votes of credit, and too large a standing army, etc.'[28] Hume here linked the standing army and the increase in public credit as threats to public liberty. In 'Of the Protestant Succession', written in 1748 but not published until

1752, Hume claimed that public liberty had continually increased in Britain since the sixteenth century, primarily because of 'the happiness of our situation, which, for a long time, gave us sufficient security, without any standing army or military establishment'. At the same time, however, public liberty in Europe had declined greatly because 'the people were disgusted at the hardships of the old feudal militia, and rather chose to entrust their prince with mercenary armies, which he easily turned against themselves'.[29] Hume considered it a great disadvantage of the protestant succession that 'A Prince, who fills the throne with a disputed title, dares not arm his subjects; the only method of securing a people fully, both against domestic oppression and foreign conquests'.[30] Moreover, when Hume designed a perfect commonwealth, he provided it with a citizen militia modelled upon the Swiss. He regarded it as 'obvious' that 'without a militia, it is in vain to think that any free government will ever have security or stability'.[31] When Hume wrote about Elizabeth's reign, he observed that, since the crown did not possess a mercenary army, and the citizens were armed, there was a 'tacit check' upon the power of the crown. He added that 'this situation of England, though seemingly it approached nearer, was in reality more remote from a despotic and eastern monarchy than the present government of that kingdom, where the people, though guarded by multiplied laws, are totally naked, defenceless, and disarmed'.[32] Such was Hume's opinion of the security and stability of public liberty in Hanoverian England. Indeed, he regarded it as a great defect in a mixed monarchy that 'The sword is in the hands of a single person, who will always neglect to discipline the militia, in order to have a pretence for keeping up a standing army'. And, up until 1769, he added that 'this is a mortal distemper in the BRITISH government, of which it must at last inevitably perish'.[33]

Everything points to Hume as the author of *Sister Peg*. It has been ascribed to Ferguson primarily on the basis of Carlyle's testimony, and we have considered reasons for rejecting that testimony. Ferguson never claimed to have written it. Hume, perhaps rashly, did acknowledge it, in a letter which reads remarkably like other letters regarding his suppressed writings. He admired the Tory wits, forcefully advocated citizen militias, wished to continue his history beyond the Revolution, and urged Wedderburn and Boswell to write a popular history of the Union of England and Scotland.[34] Moreover, Hume strongly disliked William Pitt the Elder, Robert Dundas, Lord Hardwicke, the Duke of Newcastle, and Samuel Johnson – five men who are ridiculed in *Sister Peg*; and he was the intimate friend of Sir Harry Erskine, James Oswald, and Gilbert Elliot – three Scottish Members of Parliament who are immortalized in the satire.

Why, then, did Hume suppress *Sister Peg*? The most probable answer is that he came to regard it as an inferior production. Carlyle reports that it 'excited both Admiration and Animosity' in Scotland, but the major London literary periodicals gave it a mixed reception. Smollett's *Critical Review* observed that the author is 'sometimes indecent in the expression' but praised his 'genius for portraiture': 'Had not the inimitably humorous performance of Dr Arbuthnot led the way, this little piece would be allowed to possess more merit than will now be granted by the admirers of that celebrated writer. The several nations and individuals are extremely well characterised, and the imitation happily supported.'[35] The *Monthly Review*, however, gave *Sister Peg* a devastating notice: 'A very unequal imitation of, or rather a sequel to, the admirable History of John Bull. It has neither the humour nor the style of the original; and, indeed, it is sometimes not even common English. The Author is evidently a North-Briton; not sufficiently acquainted with our language, to express himself decently in print: how great then must have been his presumption, in pretending to imitate so excellent a Pattern!'[36] In the 1760s Hume suppressed some essays because he considered them 'too frivolous for the rest, and not very agreeable neither even in that trifling manner'.[37] Several years later he told his printer that he had suppressed them 'not because they could give any Offence, but because, I thought, they could neither give Pleasure nor Instruction: They were indeed bad Imitations of the agreeable *Triffling* of Addison.'[38] It therefore seems plausible that Hume suppressed *Sister Peg* because he considered it a 'trifling Performance', a 'frivolous Composition', and a bad imitation of Arbuthnot. Hume would have been mortified by the satire's poor reception in England and would have been little consoled if he had applied to *Sister Peg* what he later told the author of another unsuccessful anti-war pamphlet: that it was published 'when the Public were intoxicated with their foolish success; and a Pamphlet, if it does not take during the first Moment, falls soon into Oblivion....'.[39] Hume was so concerned with his literary reputation and those of his friends that he sought to prevent the publication of Ferguson's *Essay* because he believed that it would be a failure and therefore damage Ferguson's reputation. 'This is a very serious Matter', he told Dr Blair. 'Any Failure of Success in this particular, besides the Mortification attending it, operates backwards, and discredits his class, which is at present in so flourishing a Situation.'[40]

A desire to protect his personal reputation would have afforded Hume an additional motive for suppressing *Sister Peg*. The caricatures of Pitt and of Dundas would have been regarded as malicious, and Hume himself advocated that questions concerning the personal character of public officials 'are of little importance to the public, and lay those, who employ their pens upon them, under a just suspicion either of malevolence or of flattery'.[41] Hume prided himself upon the distance which he had 'always kept from all Party & Dependance, from all Satyre and Panegyric'; but *Sister Peg* would have been regarded as a party piece designed to forward Lord Bute's faction.[42] Moreover, Gilbert Elliot, the main hero of the satire, might not have appreciated it at a time when he was being considered by Lord Hardwicke and the Duke of Newcastle as the man to manage Scotland, after the death of Argyll on 15 April 1761.[43]

Five of Hume's early essays are acknowledged imitations of Addison; 'The Epicurean', 'The Stoic', 'The Platonist', and 'The Sceptic' are imitations of Cicero; 'The Bellman's Petition' is in the style of Arbuthnot and Swift; the highly successful 'Character of Sir Robert Walpole' is in the style of Tacitus; the posthumously published *Dialogues concerning Natural Religion* is an imitation of Cicero's *De Natura Deorum*;[44] and Hume once considered writing modern lives after the manner of Plutarch.[45] In light of his penchant for imitating popular originals, and his 'hero-worship'[46] of Arbuthnot, it is not surprising that Hume should have composed an imitation of the *History of John Bull*, a work which has been called 'the most ingenious and humorous political satire extant in our language'.[47] Nor is it surprising that Hume should have suppressed his authorship so successfully that *Sister Peg* has never been attributed to him during the past two hundred and twenty years. After all, Hume's anonymous *A Letter from a Gentleman to his Friend in Edinburgh* (1745) was discovered only in the late 1960s; and until 1938, when Keynes and Sraffa discovered and published Hume's anonymous *An Abstract of a Treatise of Human Nature* (1740), many scholars believed that Adam Smith had written this work. What Keynes and Sraffa remark concerning the *Abstract* may, *mutatis mutandis*, be applied to *Sister Peg*: 'All is characteristic of Hume – the calculated demureness of his first appearance, the inability to resist the temptation to write and print an anonymous puff of his own work, and, when this too falls flat, a shamefaced suppression of the whole episode so completely successful that near two hundred years have passed before its rescue from oblivion.'[48]

The main topic of *Sister Peg* is the right of Scotland to have a citizen militia. In 1757 George Townshend and William Pitt managed to put through parliament a bill establishing a militia in England. Scotland was neglected in this measure, but the threat of a French invasion of the unprotected Lowlands in 1759 stimulated the Scottish Members to press for a Scottish militia. In 1760 a bill for this purpose was introduced into the House by Gilbert Elliot, but it was resoundingly defeated, largely through the opposition of Lord Hardwicke ('Nurse') and the Duke of Newcastle ('Hubble-bubble'). The first part of *Sister Peg* puts these proceedings in historical perspective. The Introduction relates the affairs of Scotland ('Peg') and England ('John Bull') from the accession of James I to the Union of Parliaments in 1707. Chapter I deals with the relations of England and France ('Lewis Baboon') and relates how their quarrel over dividing North America ('the west-common') led to the Seven Years' War. Chapter II portrays the change from citizen militias to mercenary soldiers ('gamekeepers') and considers how this change has come about in England. Chapter III relates the Jacobite Rebellion of 1745 ('that damned unnatural diabolical hell-fire scamper') and its aftermath. The French capture of Minorca ('Cracket-Island') and Pitt's rise to power in 1756 are described in Chapter IV, while the following chapter depicts John Bull coming to his senses and demanding a militia rather than Hanoverian and Hessian troops for his defence. Lord Hardwicke's fear of a citizen militia is ridiculed in Chapter VI, and the following chapter celebrates George Townshend's agitation for a militia. Chapter IX portrays the war fever consequent upon Pitt's victories against the French. Chapter X deals with the threat of a French invasion, and Scotland's petition for the right to arm her citizens. Chapter XI relates how this petition was well received by John Bull, but ignored by Pitt. The remaining six chapters give the history of the proceedings in parliament.

Whether national defence should be in the hands of a citizen militia, or left entirely to a professional army, was a hotly debated political issue in eighteenth-century Britain.[49] The invasion scares of the 1750s made many people recall how, during the Jacobite uprising of 1745, the rebellious Highlanders had triumphed so easily over the defenceless citizens of Scotland and England. It is seldom noticed that Hume himself wrote a pamphlet about their capture of Edinburgh and almost unopposed advance to Derby. One could not recall 'without Indignation and Shame', he lamented, how a small force of Highlanders

trampled down the whole Low-Countries, who were generally averse to their Cause, and whose Ancestors could have dissipated twenty times the Force of such Barbarians: They advanced into the middle of *England*, without meeting any Resistance: They threw a prodigious Alarm into the Capital itself, the greatest City in the Universe; they shook and rent the whole Fabrick of the Government, and the whole System of Credit on which it was built. And tho' there were three regular Armies in *England*, each of them much more numerous than they, they retreated back into their own Country; and still maintained their Ground. Nor can any reasonable Man doubt, that if these Armies had been removed, eight Millions of People must have been subdued and reduced to Slavery by five Thousand, the bravest, but still the most worthless amongst them.

These events demonstrated the danger of an unarmed citizenry relying for its defence upon a professional army. They also made a strong impression upon Hume:

I shall never forget the Conversation on these Events, I had at that time with a *Swiss* Gentleman, that could not sufficiently admire how so great a People, who really are Lords of the Ocean, and who boast of holding in their Hand the Ballance of Power in *Europe*, could be so impotent and defenceless against so mean a Foe, *Let those*

Highlanders, says he, *have invaded my Country, and the Militia of three* Swiss *Parishes would have repelled, what the whole Force of your three Kingdoms is scarce able to master.*

Hume added that 'this Boast contains no Exaggeration, but a serious, and, to us, a very melancholy Truth'.[50]

The third chapter of *Sister Peg* describes the Highland advance through England, or 'How John got a terrible fright in his own house of Bull-hall'. In his official history Hume had wryly observed that 'history is sometimes constrained to depart a little from her native and accustomed gravity'.[51] *Sister Peg* allowed full-rein to his urge to ridicule. The account of the '45 is prefaced with the remark that 'history, with all her gravity, will scarcely make posterity believe how much John was afraid of his own sister Margaret's garret lodgers'. After the rebels occupied Edinburgh, and defeated some British forces, John 'called out to his game-keepers, who were gone nobody knows where, then to Nicholas Frog, Rousterdivel, and all the damned names you can think of, to come to the assistance of John Bull, whose throat was just going to be cut in his own house'. This chapter illustrates the danger of relying wholly upon a professional army, and shows how John Bull had become a coward in his own house.

Arbuthnot's political allegory, with its use of national characters, provided a perfect vehicle for Hume's own preoccupations with national characters and the problems of historical change. Moreover, Arbuthnot's 'true character of John Bull' supplies the background against which the changes in John Bull's martial spirit must be viewed.

Bull, in the main, was an honest plain-dealing Fellow, Cholerick, Bold, and of a very unconstant Temper, he dreaded not Old *Lewis* either at Back-Sword, single Faulcion, or Cudgel-play; but then he was very apt to quarrel with his best Friends, especially if they pretended to govern him: If you flatter'd him, you might lead him like a Child. *John's* Temper depended very much upon the Air; his Spirits rose and fell with the Weather-glass. *John* was quick, and understood his business very well, but no Man alive was more careless, in looking into his Accounts, or more cheated by Partners, Apprentices, and Servants: This was occasioned by his being a Boon-Companion, loving his Bottle and his Diversion; for to say Truth, no Man kept a better House than *John,* nor spent his Money more generously. By plain and fair dealing, *John* had acquir'd some

Plumbs, and might have kept them, had it not been for his unhappy Law-Suit.[52]

This 'true character of John Bull' is invoked in the opening paragraph of Chapter IV in order to address the Swiss gentleman's puzzle as to how the English can be so courageous on the Ocean but so impotent at home:

We know how difficult a thing it is to write history. Whenever the reader meets with any thing that exceeds his own pitch, he presently attacks the credit of the historian; and we shall now be asked how came John Bull, who was such a coward in his own house, to be so very rash, as we have said, in that scuffle with Lewis Baboon. The fact is, that John never was slow at getting into a quarrel; he was choleric beyond measure; and as for mischief out of doors, there was nobody readier. He had a parcel of watermen who feared neither man nor devil, and when he was in his barge, either on the east or the west lake, it was but a word and a blow with him; he never was afraid to meet with Lewis Baboon there, nor any where else, except at home.

John Bull is naturally courageous, but various causes have rendered him almost impotent in his own home. In days gone by, John 'hated a sneaking, puny, pewling fellow, like the devil'; but 'people persuaded him by degrees, that if he had money enough there was nothing else worth minding. From this hopeful maxim, he even neglected sending his children to school, locked up their cudgels and cricket-batts, and would not let one of them touch a gun...' As a result, military discipline was neglected, martial spirit declined, and the people became cowards.

'It would require the pen of a great historian to tell how this great change was brought about.' The difficulty is not simply to account for the change in John Bull's martial spirit, for

some of John's neighbours were grown worse than even he was at this time. Lewis Baboon was grown from a spruce forward gallant, a mere priest-ridden, whore-ridden, flimsey periwig-making old fool. Lord Strutt could never be got out of his bed before eleven o'clock in the morning; and Nicholas Frog would rather have taken ready money for a farthing-candle, than see his best friend return from the grave. One stout man could have chaced a hundred of them into the sea, and yet these damned fellows contrived to be very troublesome for all that, by means of a device of which the devil himself was certainly the author.

In the *History of England* Hume explained how the 'habits of luxury' dissipated the fortunes of the nobles so that in some nations the kings established standing armies.[53] He elsewhere observed that when men 'have been allowed to addict themselves *entirely* to the Cultivation of Arts and Manufactures, the Habit of their Mind, still more than that of their Body, soon renders them entirely unfit for the Use of Arms. . .'.[54] In *Sister Peg* we are told that the use of mercenaries increased when John Bull, Lewis Baboon, Lord Strutt and Nicholas Frog 'grew lazy, spiritless, and purse-proud'; and that John has always had misgivings about entrusting mercenaries with his defence, but his excuse is that he 'only keep[s] them as long as Squire Geoffrey and his abettors are like to be troublesome'. But John's enemies said that he kept so many mercenaries because he was afraid without 'some of his bullies by him'. The author of *Sister Peg* insinuates that cowardice was not the *cause* of England's reliance upon mercenaries ('Whether this was the cause, or the effect of his keeping those fellows. . .'); and avoids placing the blame wholly upon commercial society. Similarly, in Hume's *History* the unwarlike disposition of the ancient Britons is represented as the *effect* of their long dependence upon the Romans for their defence and civil government. The 'monkish historians', however, ascribe to the vice of luxury, 'not to their cowardice or improvident counsels, all their subsequent calamities. So partial are all nations to themselves; and so unwilling to acknowledge that they are justly exposed to the reproach of these more dishonourable vices!'[55]

In 'Of National Characters' Hume rejected any appeal to physical causes, such as the air and climate, in order to explain the peculiar manners of each nation. Unlike Arbuthnot, Montesquieu, and Ferguson, Hume believed that national characters could be explained wholly by *moral* causes, such as 'the nature of the government, the revolution of public affairs, the plenty or penury in which the people live, the situation of the nation with regard to its neighbours, and such like circumstances'. Hume was also interested in explaining how the manners of a people change, and believed that the causes could be reduced to three: 'either by great alterations in their government, by the mixtures of new people, or by that inconstancy, to which all human affairs are subject'.[56] In this essay and in the *History* his examples are drawn from changes in martial spirit.[57] Hume observed in 'Of National Characters' that 'courage, of all national qualities, is the most precarious; because it is exerted only at intervals, and by a few in every nation...If courage be preserved, it must be by discipline, example, and opinion.'[58] Yet he believed 'that the natural propensity of men towards military shows and exercises will go far, with a little attention in the sovereign, towards exciting and supporting this [martial] spirit in any nation'.[59] But Charles II and James II were jealous of their subjects, and neglected to discipline the militia. After the Revolution the sovereigns did not dare to arm their subjects, and the situation of Great Britain, with its great naval power, continued to operate as a general cause of this neglect.[60]

In 'Of Refinement in the Arts' Hume argued that 'the ages of refinement are both the happiest and most virtuous'. He there insisted that most historians have mistaken 'the cause of the disorders in the ROMAN state, and ascribed to luxury and the arts, what really proceeded from an ill modelled government, and the unlimited extent of conquests'. In like manner, he argued against the prevalent view that increased luxury inevitably results in a decline in martial spirit.

Nor need we fear, that men, by losing their ferocity, will lose their martial spirit, or become less undaunted and vigorous in defence of their country or their liberty. The arts have no such effect in enervating either the mind or body. On the contrary, industry, their inseparable attendant, adds new force to both. And if anger, which is said to be the whetstone of courage, loses somewhat of its asperity, by politeness and refinement; a sense of honour, which is a stronger, more constant, and more governable principle, acquires fresh vigour by that elevation of genius which arises from knowledge and a good education. Add to this, that courage can neither have any duration, nor be of any use, when not accompanied with discipline and martial skill, which are seldom found among a barbarous people.

Hume relied upon Machiavelli and Guicciardini in order to counter an obvious objection:

the modern ITALIANS are the only civilized people, among EUROPEANS, that ever wanted courage and a martial spirit. Those who would ascribe this effeminacy of the ITALIANS to their luxury, or politeness, or application to the arts, need but consider the FRENCH and ENGLISH, whose bravery is as uncontestable, as their love for the arts, and their assiduity in commerce. The ITALIAN historians give us a more satisfactory reason for this degeneracy of their countrymen. They shew us how the sword was dropped at once by all the ITALIAN sovereigns, while the VENETIAN aristocracy was jealous of its subjects, the FLORENTINE democracy applied itself entirely to commerce; ROME was governed by priests, and NAPLES by women. War then became the business of soldiers of fortune, who spared one another, and to the astonishment of the world, could engage a whole day in what they called a battle, and return at night to their camp, without the least bloodshed.[61]

We have seen that as early as 1742 Hume had linked public credit and mercenary armies as dangerous threats to public liberty. No doubt he had these practices in mind when he observed that the Whigs have 'taken steps dangerous to liberty, under colour of securing the succession and settlement of the crown', but 'they have been betrayed into these steps by ignorance, or frailty, or the interests of their leaders'.[62] Although Hume regarded these two practices as equally dangerous, he considered public credit the more certain evil. 'If the abuses of treasures be dangerous, either by engaging the state in rash enterprises, or making it neglect military discipline, in confidence of its riches; the abuses of mortgaging are more certain and inevitable; poverty, impotence, and subjection to foreign powers.'[63]

The vast increases in public debt were largely due to the wars with France, and while Hume applauded the British national spirit when directed against French hegemony, he also condemned their excessive zeal. Britain's wars with France 'have always been too far pushed from obstinacy and passion'; and 'above half our wars with FRANCE, and all our public debts, are owing more to our own imprudent vehemence, than to the ambition of our neighbours'. Hume added that

we are such true combatants, that, when once engaged, we lose all concern for ourselves and our posterity, and consider only how we may best annoy the enemy. To mortgage our revenues at so deep a rate, in wars, where we were only accessories, was surely the most fatal delusion, that a nation, which had any pretension to politics and prudence, has ever yet been guilty of. That remedy of funding, if it be a remedy, and not rather a poison, ought, in all reason, to be reserved to the last extremity...[64]

Machiavelli had described a state's use of mercenaries as a poison in the body politic, and this apt metaphor may have been in Hume's mind when he penned the above words. As he observed in 'Of the Liberty of the Press', 'Slavery has so frightful an aspect to men accustomed to freedom, that it must *steal upon them by degrees*, and must disguise itself in a thousand shapes, in order to be received.'[65] According to the author of *Sister Peg*, 'people persuaded [John Bull] by degrees' to trust entirely to professional soldiers. 'Every body knows that Mr Bull has chosen this expedient with great reluctance. He was always apprehensive, that whoever was master of the only arms in a house, might soon become master of the house itself. The practice, however, stole upon him...'[66] In Hume's opinion, slavery disguised itself in the forms of reckless public credit and mercenary armies. 'Mankind are, in all ages, caught by the same baits: The same tricks, played over and over again, still trepan them. The heights of popularity and patriotism are still the beaten road to power and tyranny; flattery to treachery; standing armies to arbitrary government; and the glory of God to the temporal interest of the clergy.'[67] Hume regarded ridicule as the most effective weapon against these perennial 'tricks'. The clergy are lampooned in 'The Bellman's Petition'; the pretended patriotism of Wilkes is ridiculed in a letter to the Printer of *The London Chronicle* for February 1770; and in *Sister Peg* Hume's shafts are aimed at the patriotism of Pitt and the folly of relying upon standing armies.

Hume's antipathy towards William Pitt the Elder dates from the first appearance of his *History* in 1754.[68] There are few references to Pitt in Hume's letters before the 1760s, but in those of the late 60s and 70s the chief public villain is 'that wicked Madman, Pitt'.[69] The Pitt–Newcastle ministry of 1757 is called a 'strange motley Composition'; two years later Hume joked that a French invasion 'will probably settle the Ministry. For at present the Pits & the Legs & the Grenvilles are all going by the Ears.'[70] Hume vowed that there never was 'so formidable a Demagogue' as Pitt;[71] and, in a letter written during the Wilkes commotions of 1769, he compared Pitt to a fork-tongued snake that has fed on poisonous plants all winter. 'This Villain', he wrote, 'is to thunder against the Violation of the Bill of Rights, in not allowing the County of Middlesex the Choice of its Member. Think of the Impudence of that Fellow; and his Quackery; and his Cunning; and his Audaciousness; and judge of the Influence he will have over such a deluded Multitude.'[72]

Hume's dislike of Pitt proceeded almost as much from Pitt's character as from his abuse of the mob as an extra-parliamentary opposition. As Hume remarked to Strahan:

I think that Mr [Samuel] Johnson is a great deal too favourable to Pitt, in comparing him to Cardinal Richelieu. The Cardinal had certainly great Talents besides his Audacity: The other is totally destitute of Literature, Sense, or the Knowledge of any one Branch of public Business. What other Talent indeed has he, but that of reciting with tolerable Action and great Impudence a long Discourse in which there is neither Argument, Order, Instruction, Propriety, or even Grammar? Not to mention, that the Cardinal, with his inveterate Enmities, was also capable of Friendship: While our Cut-throat never felt either the one Sentiment or the Other.[73]

But the chief reason for Hume's antipathy towards Pitt was the increase in the public debt during the Seven Years' War. As he told Strahan in 1771:

I wish I coud have the same Idea with you of the Prosperity of our public Affairs. But when I reflect, that, from 1740 to 1761, during the Course of no more than 21 Years, while a most pacific Monarch sat on the Throne of France, the Nation ran in Debt about a hundred Millions; that the wise and virtuous Minister, Pitt, could contract more Incumbrances, in six months of an unnecessary War, than we have been able to discharge during eight Years of Peace; and that we persevere in the same frantic Maxims; I can forsee nothing but certain and speedy Ruin...In other Respects the Kingdom may be thriving ...But all this is nothing in comparison of the continual Encrease of our Debts, in every idle War, into which, it seems, the Mob of London are to rush every Minister.[74]

In comparison with these harsh remarks, Hume's portrayal of Pitt in *Sister Peg* seems mild: Pitt's extravagant oratory is mocked, his opportunism is exposed, his policy shifts are traced to an overriding desire to lead the government, and his support for a Scottish militia is shown to be lukewarm. Pitt may never have read *Sister Peg*; indeed, it was likely lost amid the flood of other anti-Pitt pamphlets, such as Israel Mauduit's *Considerations on the Present German War*. Yet when others 'confounded' Pitt, as Isaac Barré did in the House in December 1761, Hume could heartily send his 'Compliments to the Man after God's own heart, who has thus struck this Goliath'.[75]

In *My Own Life* Hume claimed that he had been 'little sus-
ceptible of Enmity'.[76] Yet *Sister Peg* is in part a somewhat
malicious attack on Robert Dundas the Younger – 'one great
dolt of a fellow, called Bumbo' – a long-time opponent of Hume
and his circle. When Hume in 1752 let his name stand for the
position of Keeper of the Advocates' Library, his candidacy was
vigorously opposed by the Lord President, Robert Dundas the
Elder, and by his son Robert Dundas the Younger, then Dean of
the Faculty of Advocates. After a prolonged struggle Hume was
elected Keeper; but two years later Robert Dundas the Younger,
then Lord Advocate, slyly attempted to remove Hume from office.
The Curators of the Library expelled three 'indecent' books
which Hume had ordered, including La Fontaine's *Contes*.
Hume regarded their expulsion as a personal insult, and wrote
to Dundas requesting that they be reinstated. Hume vowed that
'if every book not superior in merit to *La Fontaine* be expelled
the Library, I shall engage to carry away all that remains in my
pocket. I know not indeed if any will remain except our fifty
pound Bible, which is too bulky for me to carry away.'[77] But
Dundas persuaded the Curators not to retract their censure. As a
result Hume felt obliged to withdraw his request, to suffer 'the
insolence of Office', and to save his honour by retaining the position while surrendering the stipend to his friend Thomas
Blacklock, the blind poet. Hume ended this affair by predicting
that, because of the shoddy treatment which he had received
from the Faculty of Advocates, they might 'be involv'd in
Reproach & Derision; and that too very lasting; at least, if La
Fontaine's Name & mine can be suppos'd to endure'.[78] Dundas
also played a prominent role in the 'High-flyer' witch-hunt
against the Reverend John Home's tragedy *Douglas* in 1757.
These animosities were probably rekindled when, in 1760,
Dundas, alone among Scottish Members, spoke in the House of
Commons against a Scottish militia.

The most dramatic, as well as the most humorous, passages in
Sister Peg involve the lampooning of Dundas. Newcastle and
Hardwicke failed to secure any Scottish Members to speak
against a militia for Scotland

till they came to Bumbo, whom they would have tried sooner, if they
had not thought themselves sure of him, and at the same time known
what degree of credit he was likely to bring them. They had some-

times let him loose upon Mrs Bull before, to very little purpose; although for discourse he was always ready, and had stuff in his head, which might be turned into jocular sayings, serious sentences, pathetic declamations, angry ebullitions, or plaintive ditties, with equal propriety. He made the same thing pass in all these shapes, but the hearers did not know either when to laugh or cry, unless he gave them a signal, by a slap in the chops, a remarkable roar, or a doleful whine, by means of which it was dangerous to sit near him; and whether you was near him or no, the changes of his voice produced an odd sort of mounting and dipping, like the heaving of waves, and had the same effect in raising a violent inclination to vomit. They say, that he had often turned Mrs Bull's stomach, and that she always took cordials when she expected a visit from him. This being the case, he was to be employed with caution...

Dundas is depicted as a man willing to betray his native country in order to secure high office, and his speech in the House of Commons is portrayed as the price which he mistakenly believed that he had to pay for the Lord Presidency. Bumbo swears that the Scottish petition for a militia ('Peg's Letter') is a forgery perpetrated by Scottish Jacobites, and his completely incoherent speech is praised by Hume's literary rival, Samuel Johnson ('Suck-Fist'). Dundas apparently proved to be an excellent Lord President, and at the end of his life could boast that 'in steady adherence to my profession, the profits of the Bar have yielded £41,212'.[79] In 1763 Hume told a friend that the Governor and Governess of the Dauphin's children have such a bigoted character 'that a Panegyric on such a Fellow as Bumbo or Sandy Webster was more to be expected from them than one on me'; a remark which suggests that he still regarded Dundas as his mortal enemy and a vile 'religious Whig'.[80]

The final chapters of *Sister Peg* commemorate Gilbert Elliot's eloquent speech in the House of Commons on 15 April 1760. Several months earlier his brother, Captain John Elliot, had won acclaim by defeating Admiral Thurot ('Lewis Baboon's scurvy waterman') in the Irish Sea. In a letter to their father, Hume revealed how pleased he was with Gilbert's performance. 'I hope your Lordship remembers my Prophecy, that the Echo of Mr Elliot's eloquence wou'd be as loud as that of the Captain's Cannon. I think the Prophecy (tho' I pretend not to Inspiration) is now entirely fulfill'd. The Accounts we receive from all hands of your Son's Appearance in this Affair of the Militia exceed any thing of the kind we have ever heard of; and it seems to be agreed, that no Man in the House was capable of such an Exertion of Eloquence, Reason, & Magnanimity; nay, that it probably never was surpassed by any one Member.'[81]

In 'Of Eloquence' Hume lamented the decline of eloquence in modern times: England could not boast of a Cicero or a Demosthenes. He allowed that a few speakers in parliament had reached the same degree of eloquence, but this only proved that they were all mediocre orators. In Athens the orators formed the taste of the people; but in England the taste of the people formed the style of the orators. In London the people avoid the debates in parliament because they 'do not think themselves sufficiently compensated, for the losing of their dinners, by all the eloquence of our most celebrated speakers'.[82] But Hume believed that the moderns, if they tried, could excel the ancients in eloquence as well as in other areas. 'This is a field', he wrote, 'in which the most flourishing laurels may yet be gathered, if any youth of accomplished genius, thoroughly acquainted with all the polite arts, and not ignorant of public business, should appear in parliament, and accustom our ears to an eloquence more commanding and pathetic.'[83] Hume may have believed that the 38-year-old Elliot had fulfilled this prophecy too. In any case, he must have been proud that the Scottish Members had attempted to rectify a state of affairs which smacked of unequal union. If there was any inequality between England and Scotland it was an inequality of talent, and the balance was in favour of Scotland. Hume was proud that Scotland had produced so many men of genius, and that the Scots were 'the People most distinguish'd for Literature in Europe'.[84] Four years after the defeat of the Scottish Militia Bill Hume's increasing Anglophobia led him to write:

I do not believe there is one Englishman in fifty, who, if he heard that I had broke my Neck to night, woud not be rejoic'd with it. Some hate me because I am not a Tory, some because I am not a Whig, some because I am not a Christian, and all because I am a Scotsman. Can you seriously talk of my continuing an Englishman? Am I, or are you, an Englishman? Will they allow us to be so? Do they not treat with Derision our Pretensions to that Name, and with Hatred our just Pretensions to surpass & to govern them?[85]

These sentiments probably were present in some measure in

1760. No doubt he was proud that the Scottish Members had acquitted themselves so well in their unsuccessful struggle for the equal right of self-defence.

The serious side of *Sister Peg* is more than a monument to the eloquence of Elliot and other Scottish Members; it also represents Hume's attempt to influence political events. The speeches in Chapters XV and XVII marshal good arguments against the Court Whig position that a citizen militia is incompatible with a prosperous commercial society. These speeches resemble the orations of Demosthenes, whose manner Hume thought would be successful in modern assemblies, if it could be copied: 'It is rapid harmony, exactly adjusted to the sense: It is vehement reasoning, without any appearance of art: It is disdain, anger, boldness, freedom, involved in a continued stream of argument.'[86] Whether they were intended to imitate Demosthenes, at least they are free from that disorderliness which Hume found in most English orators, for they conspicuously follow a method so that 'the arguments rise naturally from one another, and will retain a more thorough persuasion, than can arise from the strongest reasons, which are thrown together in confusion'.[87] These speeches are all the more forceful because one precedes, and the other follows, the farcical speech of Bumbo.

In the 1741 'Character of Robert Walpole' Hume asserted that under this minister 'trade has flourished, liberty declined, and learning gone to ruin'.[88] As instances of the decline of liberty Hume cited 'the increase of the civil list, votes of credit, and too large a standing army, etc.'. But by 1748 he had changed his mind and believed instead 'that the not paying more of our public debts was, as hinted in this character, a great, and the only great error in that long administration'.[89] We may infer from this change that in retrospect Hume judged that the standing army was not so large as to be a danger to public liberty, whereas the system of public credit and national debt posed a real threat to the well-being of Britain. We may also infer that Hume did not totally condemn standing armies, but rather condemned the extreme of a people wholly relying upon professional soldiers for their security. Similarly, the author of *Sister Peg* warns against 'the extremes, to which our maxims and our practices may finally carry us', rather than condemning standing armies outright, and argues for the establishment of a militia so that 'instead of augmenting our game-keepers, we [should be] satisfied with a moderate number in ordinary times, and prepare this resource for ourselves, against any sudden alarm'.[90] Thus Hume adopted a moderate stance on the debate over the standing army, disagreeing with the extremes of both Court and Country positions. He would have rejected as frivolous any attempt to determine the proper size of the standing army. 'All questions concerning the proper medium between extremes are difficult to be decided', he maintained, 'both because it is not easy to find *words* proper to fix this medium, and because the good and ill, in such cases, run so gradually into each other, as even to render our *sentiments* doubtful and uncertain'.[91]

Hume sided with the Court Whigs on the need for parliamentary patronage in a mixed government, while recognizing that it might ultimately lead to the easy death or 'euthanasia' of the British constitution.[92] But he rejected outright the Court Whig system of public credit and national debt, for he believed that such a system would certainly lead to the ruin of Britain: 'either the nation must destroy public credit, or public credit will destroy the nation'.[93] Hume regarded the modern practice of irresponsibly contracting public debt as a 'source of degeneracy' in free governments, just as he regarded mercenary armies as necessarily destructive of enormous monarchies. In such monarchies the nobility never will serve at remote frontiers. 'The arms of the state, must, therefore, be entrusted to mercenary strangers, without zeal, without attachment, without honour; ready on every occasion to turn them against the prince, and join each desperate malcontent, who offers pay and plunder.' Here Hume's prediction is based upon the maxim that what has been, will be again. 'The troops are filled with CRAVATES and TARTARS, HUSSARS and COSSACS; intermingled, perhaps, with a few soldiers of fortune from the better provinces: And the melancholy fate of the ROMAN emperors, from the same cause, is renewed over and over again, till the final dissolution of the monarchy.'[94]

The 'character' of professional soldiers as delineated in *Sister Peg* is such as almost to guarantee disloyalty: '. . . they are set apart from the rest of the family, and by their manner of life, are made to shake off all connection with them as much as possible . . . that they may be at all times ready to. . . do anything that their profession may require, without any regret of their own. . .

They are taught, for the same reason, to obey their leader implicitly, and to know no law but his commands; to all which conditions they bind themselves for life...'[95] As *Sister Peg* bears comparison with Hume's most pessimistic and most alarmist essay, 'Of Public Credit', so this 'character' of professional soldiers should be compared with the 'character' of stock-holders in that essay, where they are envisaged as being the only powerful citizens in the 'unnatural state' of a free society mortgaged to the limit:

These are men, who have no connexions with the state, who can enjoy their revenue in any part of the globe in which they chuse to reside...and who will sink into the lethargy of a stupid and pampered luxury, without spirit, ambition, or enjoyment. Adieu to all ideas of nobility, gentry, and family. The stocks can be transferred in an instant, and being in such a fluctuating state, will seldom be transmitted during three generations from father to son. Or were they to remain ever so long in one family, they convey no hereditary authority or credit to the possessor; and by this means, the several ranks of men, which form a kind of independent magistracy in a state, instituted by the hand of nature, are entirely lost; and every man in authority derives his influence from the commission alone of the sovereign. No expedient remains for preventing or suppressing insurrections, but mercenary armies: No expedient at all remains for resisting tyranny: Elections are swayed by bribery and corruption alone: And the middle power between king and people being totally removed, a grievous despotism must infallibly prevail.[96]

Hume's zealous advocacy of citizen militias places him in the civic humanist tradition, for he was concerned in part with the effect of institutions on individuals.[97] He firmly believed that virtue 'can never arise from the most refined precepts of philosophy, or even the severest injunctions of religion; but must proceed entirely from the virtuous education of youth, the effect of wise laws and institutions'.[98] In this respect, Hume diverged sharply from the naive views of 'severe moralists' such as John 'Estimate' Brown, who preached virtue and stridently warned that the distant ill consequences to the public welfare of apparently innocent habits or private virtues are easily overlooked: 'Many of the pernicious Effects of Luxury and Effeminacy fall under this Observation: And hence came the poor and wretched Reasonings of two Champions of Luxury and Effeminacy...'[99]

This was not the first time that Hume had been yoked with
Mandeville; yet it is ironical to find Hume accused of neglecting
the distant ill consequences of certain habits and practices, in
light of his theory of government as a 'remedy' to man's incur-
able weakness of preferring frivolous present interests to important remote interests.[100] In 'Of Refinement in the Arts', Hume
defended luxury but attempted to dissociate himself from
Mandeville by conceding that luxury 'when carried a degree too
far, is a quality pernicious, though perhaps not the most pernicious, to political society'.[101] However, the limited extent of
this concession is evident from Hume's concluding remark that
the magistrate 'cannot cure every vice by substituting a virtue in
its place. Very often he can only cure one vice by another; and
in that case, he ought to prefer what is least pernicious to society.
Luxury, when excessive, is the source of many ills; but is in
general preferable to sloth and idleness, which would commonly
succeed in its place, and are more hurtful both to private persons
and to the public.'[102]

We have already noted Hume's opinion that cowardice is a
'more dishonorable' vice than luxury. A similar point is made
in the last speech of *Sister Peg*: 'There is no vice, which may not
be grafted on cowardice, as successfully as upon avarice itself,
that other stock which we are so willing to cultivate.'[103]
Hardwicke's avarice is forgiven, but his policy is condemned;
and the self-interest of Pitt and Dundas is attacked because it
threatens public liberty. Hume believed that parliamentary 'corruption' or 'dependence' is essential to the British mixed government – '*some* degree and *some* kind of it are inseparable from
the very nature of the constitution' – but he also allowed that it
could become 'too forcible', presumably as in the use of the
standing army as a vehicle of political patronage.[104] 'Did we
resolve to try what the utmost corruption could do, to debase,
to sink and destroy a race of men, a more ingenious contrivance
could not be found than this we are disposed to follow.'[105] Hume
is usually seen as a staunch supporter of the Court, but he recog-
nized that sometimes one ought to oppose its encroachments. As
he wrote in his last essay, 'Of the Origin of Government':

liberty is the perfection of civil society; but still authority must be
acknowledged essential to its very existence: and in those contests,
which so often take place between the one and the other, the latter

27

may, on that account, challenge the preference. Unless perhaps one may say (and it may be said with some reason) that a circumstance, which is essential to the existence of civil society, must always support itself, and needs be guarded with less jealousy, than one that contributes to its perfection, which the indolence of men is so apt to neglect, or their ignorance to overlook.[106]

It was almost incumbent upon Hume to argue against the Court Whig position in order to show that virtue and commerce are compatible. The institution of a citizen militia will foster courage and other martial virtues, as the practices of the Court Whigs now encourage cowardice and hence threaten the security and stability of public liberty. Oliver Cromwell and the Civil War were never far from Hume's view of public affairs. In Chapter XV of *Sister Peg* a standing army is portrayed as

the most dangerous quarter, into which the spirit of domestic faction can come. Here is an order of men, who are always in readiness to act, whose leader is always prepared; in possession at all times of great power, and at all times desirous of more. Other factions may lurk under-ground in the seed, or spring into view to be crushed as they appear. But this is at all times a full grown plant. There needs no giant to tear it from the roots, nor is there any great address required, with the help of this weapon, to confound and destroy all the civil and domestic institutions of men.

The final chapters of *Sister Peg* constitute an elegant statement of the radical Whig critique of standing armies, and a forceful plea for equal treatment of Scotland in re-establishing a citizen militia. But Hume's plea fell on deaf ears; Scotland did not get a militia during his lifetime. Nevertheless, Hume's little work may have influenced one other political theorist. Adam Smith possessed a copy of *Sister Peg*, and in *The Wealth of Nations* he advocated a professional military establishment together with a militia.[107] It has been suggested by Duncan Forbes that Hume himself eventually and reluctantly came to agree with Smith on this issue, for in the last edition of the *History* Hume added that it seems 'a melancholy truth' that 'the magistrate must either possess a large revenue and a military force, or enjoy some discretionary powers, in order to execute the laws and support his own authority'.[108] However, this may not represent a dramatic change, for even in the 1740s Hume tolerated a moderate sized standing army as one of the 'inconveniences' of a limited monarchy. Therefore, it appears that Hume believed that ideally the radical Whig position of relying entirely upon a citizen militia is the best policy, just as a republic is ideally the best form of government; yet he also maintained that a republican Britain would be undesirable, and we may perhaps understand him as meaning that it is a 'melancholy truth' that a standing army is necessary given the established form of government in Britain, a disputed crown in the 1740s, and the 'licentiousness' of the English in the 1770s. Hume probably would have described the difference between himself and Smith on this issue as merely verbal because one of degree, with himself insisting most on the dangers of a standing army, and Smith insisting most on the necessity of employing one.[109]

'It is a strange inclination we have to be wits, preferably to every thing else', Hume once wrote.[110] In a similar vein, he confessed that he 'would give more to be thought a good Droll, than to have the Praises of Erudition, & Subtility, & Invention'. Most fortunately he was able to combine these virtues in *Sister Peg*, a work which is as entertaining as it is instructive. The detached wit of Arbuthnot's *History of John Bull* obviously suited Hume's urbane temperament. And because Hume, unlike Arbuthnot, was concerned with posterity, the density of historical allusion of Arbuthnot's allegory is missing from its sequel, so that *Sister Peg* can be read by us with little annotation. Gibbon called Hume the Scottish Tacitus; but after reading the following text one might feel inclined to call Hume the Scottish Machiavelli.

NOTES TO INTRODUCTION

S.P.: Sister Peg

1 Hume to Lord Elibank, 2 April 1759, *Texas Studies in Literature and Language*, 4 (1962), 448.
2 Hume signed an agreement with his publisher 27 July 1759. The next day he wrote to Adam Smith: 'It is chiefly as a Resource against Idleness, that I shall undertake this Work: For as to Money, I have enough: And as to Reputation, what I have wrote already will be sufficient, if it be good: If not, it is not likely I shall now write better. I found it impracticable (at least fancy'd

so) to write the History since the Revolution.' *The Letters of David Hume*, ed. J. Y. T. Greig, 2 vols. (Oxford, 1932), 1.

3 Hume to Andrew Millar, 22 March 1760, *Letters*, I, 321.

4 George Murray to James Murray, 3 March 1761; quoted in Ernest Mossner, *The Life of David Hume* (Oxford, 1980), 238. In the Index the publication is referred to as 'Gowler' and is listed under the heading 'Works, published but still unlocated'.

5 Hume to Lord Elibank, 8 Jan. 1748, *Texas Studies*, 4 (1962), 437f.

6 The 1750 skit is known as 'The Petition of the Patients of Westminster against James Fraser, apothecary' and is printed in *Letters*, II, 340–2; Hume wrote that 'it is very witty. I contriv'd it one night, that I coud not sleep for the Tortures of Rheumatisms' (*Letters*, I, 142). The unlocated 1751 skit is entitled 'A Letter to a certain turbulent Patriot in Westminster, from a Friend in the Country'.

7 Hume to John Clephane, 18 Feb. 1751, *Letters*, I, 149.

8 Hume to Gilbert Elliot, 18 Feb. 1751, *Letters*, I, 153. 'The Bellman's Petition' resembles in several respects Arbuthnot's 'Reasons Humbly Offered by the Company exercising the Trade and Mystery of Upholders, against part of the Bill for the Better Viewing, Searching, and Examining Drugs, Medicines, &c.'.

9 Hume to Gilbert Elliot, 10 March 1751, *Letters*, I, 156f.

10 Hume to Alexander Carlyle, 3 Feb. 1761, *Letters*, II, 341f.

11 Henry MacKenzie in *The Works of John Home, Esq.*, ed. H. MacKenzie, 3 vols. (Edinburgh, 1822), I, 25f., 154f.; *The Life and Correspondence of David Hume*, ed. J. Hill Burton, 2 vols. (Edinburgh, 1846), II, 88; J. Y. T. Greig, *David Hume* (London, 1931), 261; Mossner, *Life*, 285; David Kettler, *The Social and Political Thought of Adam Ferguson* (Ohio, 1965), 73 n.32.

12 *An Argument to prove that the tragedy of Douglas ought to be publickly burned by the hands of the hangman.* Edinburgh, 1757. *Plain Reasons for Removing a Certain Great Man from His M——y's Presence and Councils for ever. Addressed to the people of England.* By O. M. Haberdasher. London, 1759. Extracts of this pamphlet appeared in the *Scots Magazine*, 21 (1759), 165f. *The Question relating to a Scots Militia considered...By a Freeholder.* Edinburgh, 1760. This pamphlet was reprinted twice in London with a preface by George Townshend, and an extract was printed in the *Scots Magazine*, 22 (1760), 53–6. Hume said it 'was certainly wrote with Spirit' (*Letters*, I, 322).

13 Alexander Carlyle, *Anecdotes and Characters of the Times*, ed. J. Kinsley (Oxford, 1973), 140, 206f.

14 Mossner, *Life*, 277, 338.
15 *Letters*, I, 410f.
16 John Ramsay of Ochtertyre, *Scotland and Scotsmen in the Eighteenth Century*, ed. A. Allardyce, 2 vols. (Edinburgh, 1888), I, 334n.
17 Of Ferguson's *The Morality of Stage-plays Seriously Considered* (1757) a contemporary observed that 'the stile and manner of it is very poor and dull, so that I am positive the author cannot be a man of genius'. *Diary of George Ridpath, 1755–1761* (Edinburgh, 1922). 126. Duncan Forbes writes:

> The poet Gray described [Ferguson's] style as 'short-winded and sententious', and on the whole this is a fair criticism. The *Essay* cannot be described as a literary masterpiece though it has its moments...Ferguson has not achieved the mastery of the foreign language shown by Hume, Smith or Robertson. It is not always easy to discover exactly what he is saying; suddenly he will be off on a new tack, sometimes between one sentence and the next. Adam Ferguson, *An Essay on the History of Civil Society*, ed. Duncan Forbes (Edinburgh, 1966), xxivf.

18 *Reflections Previous to the Establishment of a Militia* (Edinburgh, 1756), last paragraph.
19 Hume to Hugh Blair, 11 Feb. 1766, *Letters*, II, 12; cf. 132.
20 In the famous Douglas Cause of the 1760s Hume believed that it had been 'made clear even in the Eyes the most blinded & most prejudiced' that the Douglas claim rested upon an imposture. Hume concluded a letter to Carlyle of 15 Sept. 1763 by asking: 'Pray is there any body such an Idiot at present as to be a Partizan of the Douglas?' (*Letters*, I, 397f.) Hume would have known that Carlyle was a zealous supporter of the Douglas claim.
21 Hume to Adam Smith, 28 July 1759, *Letters*, I, 314.
22 Hume to William Strahan, 25 Jan. 1772, *Letters*, II, 253f.
23 *Letters*, I, 12–18; Mossner, 'Hume's Epistle to Dr Arbuthnot, 1734: The Biographical Significance', *Huntington Library Quarterly*, VII (1944), 135–52; Mossner, *Life*, 84.
24 *New Letters*, 184f.
25 J. G. A. Pocock, 'Hume and the American Revolution: The Dying Thoughts of a North Briton', in D. F. Norton, N. Capaldi, and W. L. Robison, eds., *McGill Hume Studies* (San Diego, 1980), 341.
26 Duncan Forbes, *Hume's Philosophical Politics* (Cambridge, 1976), 212.
27 *History*, VII, 150.
28 Mossner, *Life*, 144.
29 *Essays*, I, 472. (*Essays* I and II correspond to *Philosophical Works* III and IV).

30 *Essays*, I, 476.
31 *Essays*, I, 490.
32 *History*, V, 409.
33 *Essays*, I, 491.
34 James Boswell, *Boswell: The Ominous Years, 1774—1776*, eds. C. Ryskamp and F. A. Pottle (New York, 196), 29f.
35 *The Critical Review*, x (1760), 451–3. Lester Beattie also judged that the author's 'powers of characterization were of a high order' and added that 'the first half of the allegory is compact, full of incident, and racy', whereas 'the last chapters are marred by long arguments'. *John Arbuthnot: Mathematician and Satirist* (Cambridge, Mass., 1935), 185f.
36 *The Monthly Review, or, Literary Journal*, XXIV (1761), 165.
37 Hume to Adam Smith, 24 Sept. 1752, *Letters*, I, 168.
38 Hume to Strahan, 7 Feb. 1772, *Letters*, II, 257.
39 Hume to Turgot, 8 July 1768, *Letters*, II, 183; the pamphlet here referred to is Josiah Tucker's *The Case of going to war for the sake of procuring, enlarging, or securing of Trade, considered in a new light* (London, 1763).
40 Hume to Blair, 11 Feb. 1766, *Letters*, II, 13.
41 *Essays*, I, 109.
42 Hume to the Abbé LeBlanc, 12 Sept. 1754, *Letters*, I, 193:
This consideration is suggested by Hume's ironical remark in a cryptic letter to Strahan of late 1760 or early 1761: 'I was glad to observe what our King says, that Faction is at an End and Party Distinctions abolish'd. You may infer from this, that I think I have kept clear of Party in my History; that I think I have been much injurd when any thing of that Nature has been imputed to me...' *Letters*, I, 336.

John Almon relates that King George III and his Leicester House advisors intended 'to remove the ministers, and conclude the war; but the tide of popularity ran so strong in favour of both, they were obliged to postpone the execution of their design, until they had prepared the nation to receive it. For this purpose, a great number of writers were employed to calumniate the late King, the Duke of *Cumberland*, Mr Pitt, and all the Whigs'. Almon adds that '*Smollett, Mallett, Francis, Home, Murphy, Mauduit*, and many others, were the instruments employed upon this occasion.' *Anecdotes of the Life of the Right Hon. William Pitt, Earl of Chatham*, 7th ed. (London, 1810), I, 261–4. For an account of this pamphlet literature see John Brewer, *Party Ideology and Popular Politics at the Accession of George III* (Cambridge, 1976). Brewer does not mention *Sister Peg*.

J. G. A. Pocock writes: 'Hume had always been careful not to carry his *History* into the era between 1688 and his own time, or to give his analysis of recent and contemporary British politics. But his acquaintance Tobias Smollett, the London Scot, had not hesitated to publish an avowed continuation of Hume's *History*, in which he analyzed post-Revolution Britain in terms more Tory, Country, and anticommercial than Hume would have permitted himself. This had left him in the role of professional apologist for Lord Bute and the young George III; and faced with the anti-Scottish frenzies of *The North Briton*, Smollett had been destroyed.' 'Hume and the American Revolution', *McGill Hume Studies*, 338f.

43 Sir Lewis Namier and John Brooke, eds., *The House of Commons 1745–1790*, 3 vols. (London, 1964), II, 392.

44 Christine Battersby, 'The *Dialogues* as Original Imitation: Cicero and the Nature of Hume's Scepticism', in D. F. Norton, N. Capaldi, and W. L. Robinson, eds., *McGill Hume Studies* (San Diego, 1980), 239–52.

45 Hume to Robertson, 7 April 1759, *Letters*, I, 315f.

46 Mossner, *Life*, 86.

47 T. B. Macaulay, *The History of England from the Accession of James the Second* (London, 1915), VI, 2848.

48 *An Abstract of a Treatise of Human Nature, 1740: A Pamphlet hitherto unknown by David Hume.* Reprinted with an Introduction by J. M. Keynes and P. Sraffa (Cambridge, 1938).

49 For a good account of this issue see J. R. Western, *The English Militia in the Eighteenth Century: The Story of a Political Issue, 1660–1802* (London, 1965); and J. G. A. Pocock, *The Machiavellian Moment* (Princeton, 1975), chaps. X–XIV.

50 *Account of Stewart*, 10ff.

51 Hume, *The History of Great Britain: The Reigns of James I and Charles I*, ed. D. Forbes (Harmondsworth, 1970), 147.

52 The enlargement of commerce and navigation increased industry and the arts every where; the nobles dissipated their fortunes in expensive pleasures; men of an inferior rank both acquired a share in the landed property, and created to themselves a considerable property of a new kind, in stock, commodities, art, credit, and correspondence. In some nations, the privileges of the commons increased by this increase of property: in most nations, the kings, finding arms to be dropped by the barons, who could no longer endure their former rude manner of life, established standing armies, and subdued the liberties of their kingdoms; but in all places the condition of the people, from the depression of the petty tyrants by whom they had formerly been oppressed rather than governed, received great improvement; and they acquired, if not entire liberty, at least the most considerable advantages of it. *History*, IV, 398; cf. V, 427f.

53 John Arbuthnot, *The History of John Bull*, ed. Bower and Erikson (Oxford, 1976), 9.
54 *Account of Stewart*, 7f.; italics added.
55 *History*, vi, 118. The last sentence is scored out in Hume's MS. and was never printed. See the Hume MSS. in the Royal Society of Edinburgh, x.
56 *Essays*, i, 244, 248f.
57 The old SPANIARDS were restless, turbulent, and so addicted to war, that many of them killed themselves, when deprived of their arms by the ROMANS. One would find an equal difficulty at present...to rouze up the modern SPANIARDS to arms. The BATAVIANS were all soldiers of fortune, and hired themselves into the ROMAN armies. Their posterity make use of foreigners for the same purpose that the ROMANS did their ancestors. *Essays*, i, 250f.

In arguing that the Irish and the Scots Highlanders were the same race, Hume wrote:

It is in vain to argue against these facts from the supposed warlike disposition of the Highlanders, and unwarlike of the ancient Irish. Those arguments are still much weaker than the authorities. Nations change very quickly in these particulars. The Britons were unable to resist the Picts and Scots, and invited over the Saxons for their defence, who repelled those invaders; yet the same Britons valiantly resisted, for a hundred and fifty years, not only this victorious band of Saxons, but infinite numbers more, who poured in upon them from all quarters. Robert Bruce, in 1322, made a peace, in which England, after many defeats, was constrained to acknowledge the independence of his country; yet in no more distant period than ten years after, Scotland was totally subdued by a small handful of English, led by a few private noblemen. All history is full of such events. *History*, i, 26f.

58 *Essays*, i, 255.
59 *History*, vi, 118.
60 *History*, vii, 383; viii, 314; *Essays*, i, 476.
61 *Essays*, i, 304.
62 *Essays*, i, 141, 476f.
63 *Essays*, i, 362.
64 *Essays*, i, 354.
65 *Essays*, i, 95; italics added.
66 See below, *S.P.*, 93.
67 *Essays*, i, 372f.
68 Mossner, *Life*, 310.
69 Hume to Strahan, 26 Oct. 1775, *Letters*, ii, 301.
70 *Letters*, i, 253, 307.
71 Hume to Baron Mure, 1 Sept. 1763, *Letters*, i, 393.
72 Hume to Hugh Blair, 28 March 1769, *Letters*, ii, 197f.

73 Hume to Strahan, 25 March 1771, *Letters*, II, 242.
74 Hume to Strahan, 11 March 1771, *Letters*, II, 237.
75 Hume to Robert Clerk, 12 Dec. 1761, *New Letters*, 65.
76 *Essays*, I, 8. In an open letter to Strahan, Adam Smith remarked that Hume's 'constant pleasantry was the genuine effusion of good-nature, and without even the slightest tincture of malignity, so frequently the disagreeable source of what is called wit in other men'. *Essays*, I, 13.
77 Hume to Robert Dundas, 20 Nov. 1754, *Letters*, I, 212.
78 Hume to Robert Dundas, (?) Nov. 1754, *Forum for Modern Language Studies*, VI (1970), 352.
79 Quoted in *The Arniston Memoirs*, ed. G. W. T. Omond (Edinburgh, 1887), 168.
80 Hume to William Robertson, 1 Dec. 1763, *New Letters*, 75f. The Reverend Alexander Webster (1707–84), nicknamed 'Dr Bonum Magnum', was one of the leaders of the 'High-flyer' witch-hunt against John Home's *Douglas*. The distinction between political and religious Whigs is made in the Postscript to the *Account of Stewart*: A political Whig is 'a Man of Sense and Moderation, a Lover of Laws and Liberty, whose chief Regard to particular Princes and Families, is founded on a Regard to the publick Good'. But a zeal for the Book of Common-Prayer, 'when mixt up with Party Notions', produces a 'poison in human Beasts': 'Dissimulation, Hypocrisy, Violence, Calumny, Selfishness are, generally speaking, the true and legitimate Offspring of this kind of Zeal.' However, the religious Whigs,

whatever they may imagine, form but the Fag-end of the Party, and are, at the Bottom, very heartily despised by their own Leaders. Once on a time, indeed, the Breech got above the Head; when *Cromwel*, *Ireton*, *Warriston*, &c. ruled our Councils and Armies; and then there was fine Work indeed. But ever since, though their Assistance has been taken at Elections, and they have been allowed, in Return, to rail and make a Noise as much as they please, they have had but little Influence on our publick Determinations; and long may it continue so.

81 Hume to Lord Minto, 1 May 1760, *Letters*, I, 325.
82 *Essays*, I, 165.
83 *Essays*, I, 172.
84 Hume to Gilbert Elliot, 2 July 1757, *Letters*, I, 255.
85 Hume to Gilbert Elliot, 22 Sept. 1764, *Letters*, I, 470. Eight days later Hume wrote to Elliot: 'I spoke to you with great Freedom, and am infinitely uneasy lest my letter [of 22 Sept. 1764] should fall into bad hands.' *Letters*, I, 471.

86 *Essays*, I, 170.
87 *Essays*, I, 174.
88 *Essays*, II, 396.
89 *Essays*, I, 45.
90 See below, *S.P.*, 101, 94
91 *Essays*, I, 121.
92 *Essays*, I, 126.
93 *Essays*, I, 370.
94 *Essays*, I, 355f.
95 See below, *S.P.*, 93.
96 *Essays*, I, 367f.
97 For an account of civic humanism see Pocock, *The Machiavellian Moment* and Quentin Skinner, *The Foundations of Modern Political Thought*, 2 vols. (Cambridge, 1978).
98 *Essays*, I, 127.
99 John Brown, *An Estimate of the Manners and Principles of the Times*, 2 vols. (London, 1758), II, 174. Of this work Hume told his publisher, Andrew Millar: 'I doubt not but I could easily refute Dr Brown; but as I had taken a Resolution never to have the least Altercation with these Fellows, I shall not readily be brought to pay any Attention to him.' Brown 'is a Flatterer... of that low Fellow, Warburton. And any thing so low as Warburton, or his Flatterers, I should certainly be ashamd to engage with.' Hume asked Millar to read this letter to Dr Brown as being 'all the Answer I shall ever deign to give him'. Hume to Millar, 20 May 1757, *Letters*, I, 250.
100 *A Treatise of Human Nature*, Book III, Pt. II, Sec. 7.
101 *Essays*, I, 300.
102 *Essays*, I, 309. F. A. Hayek has argued that Mandeville 'made Hume possible': 'It is only in Hume's work that the significance of Mandeville's efforts becomes wholly clear, and it was through Hume that he exercised his most lasting influence.' 'Dr Bernard Mandeville', in *Proceedings of the British Academy*, LII (1966), 139.
103 See below, *S.P.*, 101.
104 *Essays*, I, 120f., italics added; *History*, VIII, 103.
105 See below, *S.P.*, 102.
106 *Essays*, I, 116f.
107 A copy of *Sister Peg* bearing Smith's bookplate was in 1934 in the possession of Dr Piero Sraffa of Cambridge University (see *The Economic Journal*, XLVI (1936), 179). For the interpretation of Smith's views on the present issue I am greatly indebted to Donald Winch, *Adam Smith's Politics: An Essay in Historiographic Revision* (Cambridge, 1978), chap. 5.

108 Duncan Forbes, *Hume's Philosophical Politics*, 172.

109 See Hume's conciliatory remark in his *Dialogues concerning Natural Religion*, Part XII:

> It seems evident, that the dispute between the sceptics and dogmatists is entirely verbal, or at least regards only the degrees of doubt and assurance, which we ought to indulge with regards to all reasoning: And such disputes are commonly at the bottom, verbal, and admit not of any precise determination. No philosophical dogmatist denies, that there are difficulties both with regard to the senses and to all science: and that these difficulties are in a regular, logical method, absolutely insolveable. No sceptic denies, that we lie under an absolute necessity, notwithstanding these difficulties, of thinking, and believing, and reasoning with regard to all kinds of subjects, and even of frequently assenting with confidence and security. The only difference, then, between these sects, if they merit that name, is, that the sceptic, from habit, caprice, or inclination, insists most on the difficulties; the dogmatist, for like reasons, on the necessity.

110 Hume to the Comtesse de Boufflers, 12 Jan. 1766, *Letters*, II, 10.

NOTE ON THE TEXT

The copy-text is that of the second edition, which differs little from the first edition. A few obvious typographical errors have been silently corrected, and occurrences of 'Mr Luchar' have been changed to 'MacLurchar', in accordance with the erratum note in the first edition. Inverted commas and apostrophes have been imposed where they were occasionally omitted in the original, but no attempt has been made to standardize or modernize spelling, punctuation or capitalization.

The history of the
proceedings in the case of
MARGARET,
Commonly called
PEG
only lawful sister to
JOHN BULL, esq.

PRINTED FOR W. OWEN, NEAR TEMPLE BAR
MDCCLXI.

PRINCIPAL CHARACTERS

John Bull	The English people
Peg	The Scottish people
Squire Geoffrey	James II and his heirs
Sir Thomas	The King of England
Sir Humphrey Polisworth	Dr John Arbuthnot
Jack	The Church of Scotland
Lewis Baboon	The French people
Lord Strutt	The Spanish people
Squire South	The Austrian people
Nicholas Frog	The Dutch people
Nurse	Philip Yorke, first Earl of Hardwicke, Lord Chancellor
Rousterdivel	Hanoverian and Hessian soldiers
MacLurchar	Scottish Highlanders
Bumbo	Robert Dundas of Arniston
Mrs Bull	The British parliament
Hubble-bubble	Thomas Pelham, Duke of Newcastle
Jowler	William Pitt, later Earl of Chatham
Boy George	George Townshend, M.P. for Norfolk 1747–64

THE CONTENTS

45

There being no history with which every learned reader is better acquainted in general, than that of John Bull, and his sister Peg, we shall spend very little time in preambles or introductions to the present story. John and his sister lived many a day, as every body knows, in the two adjoining houses which were left them by their father; and it matters not now to say, how much better John was lodged than his sister, and how many more improvements he had made on his farm. We never heard of any difference arising between them on this score, farther than some jeers and taunts between the blackguards or scullions of either house, who generally got themselves bloody noses upon the occasion. As for Peg herself, she was so far from complaining of her portion, that nothing could offend her more, than to be told out of doors, that she was not the richest heiress in the world.

It is not easy to say, whether it was Peg's own temper, the badness of her subjects, or the perpetual vexations she met with in her youth, that hindered her from minding her domestic affairs, so much as she should have done: but the truth is, that matters were often at sixes and sevens in her family; and her brother and she, to be sure, never could agree about any thing. All the world knows how long their affairs remained in confusion, merely because they would not employ the same attorney, and what an aversion they had to trust their affairs in common to any single person. Peg would say, 'I'll have nothing to do with John's lawyers; whoever I employ must mind nobody's affairs but mine. I have as good a right to be served as he; and if he pays more than I do, let it be for services done to himself, not for cheating me.' John again would swagger and swear, and said, that whoever Peg employed, must be a dirty lousy fellow; and would come to no terms, unless she would take a steward of his choosing.

It happened, however, at last, as every careful peruser of history knoweth, that every man of the law, within the reach almost of John's knowledge, from the master down to the merest clerk-boy, died, or left the country, or disappeared some how or other, and John was obliged for once to put his papers in the hands of his sister's lawyer,[1] a very book-learned man, as many people affirm even unto this day. But be this as it will, Peg had the vanity to boast, that though her lawyer now lived in John's own house, yet it was she who gave that clod-pated pock-puddened numskull the lawyer at last; and that this same man of the law, if he had any gratitude to the house where he was born and bred, would not let her be wronged, or forget her boys, when the stock came to be divided. She trusted too, that they would remember themselves, and if John or the attorney pretended to cheat them, she talked no less than of beating out both their brains. John was really at bottom a good-natured fellow, and knowing himself to be an overmatch for Peg, did not mind her peevish humours a rush; but he would not have liked her attorney for all that, if he had not expected to manage him, by keeping him in his own house, and by putting clerks about him, who never had any connexion with Margaret, or her hungry loons,[2] from whom, the truth is, he expected no good.

This affair being settled between the brother and sister, as well as could be expected with so little cordiality on either side, their common concerns began to be a little better managed, and people got some rest in their beds; for they did not harbour vagrants,[3] as they used to do, to hamstring one another's cattle, to tear up the young planting, and knock out one another's brains. They differed, it is true, now and then about this thing, and t'other thing, and about attornies and agents, but it always happened that they employed the same person, even whilst John wished Peg at the bottom of the sea; and Peg sometimes let devilish knocks at him, and the attorney too, when she was jealous of either.

John, however, was so far lucky, that his sister concurred with him very readily in most things of consequence, such as running off Squire Geoffry, and the like; insomuch, that he himself was not readier to part with this Squire, as every body knows, although he claimed kindred to Peg, as the fostermother of his family; and to make all sure, she put her hand as freely to the perpetual contract with Sir Thomas.[4] This was a gentleman in the neighbourhood,[5] of an ancient family, and a pretty fortune of his own: but he was willing to take charge of the brother and sister's affairs, provided he had some security that he should not be turned out the next moment, which was accordingly granted in the form of a contract, by virtue of which he continues to manage their business in a very orderly regular manner.

This, however, did not hinder some persons in both families, who had a hankering after Squire Geoffry, from being mad enough once and again, to think of restoring him to his office, in spite of John's and Margaret's teeth. They came sometimes from the garret, and from the cellar, roaring about this matter; and when they got drunk, they imagined nothing was easier to be done. The truth is, that if Peg had not been firm to the contract, John would often have been sore beset.

Although the intention of this proem is far from being to give a full account of the affairs of these two families, preceding the present transaction, much less to censure or run down other grave historians, who have published to the learned world any part of their history; yet we cannot altogether pass in silence some few mistakes in the otherwise elaborate work of the celebrated Sir Humphrey Polisworth, bred in the learned university of Grub-street. An historian, in our opinion, should be as mindful of truth in whatever he may occasionally mention, as he is in the main series of his story. For want of attending to this truth, the learned Sir Humphrey has unguardedly misrepresented the nature of John's and Peg's agreement, together with the causes which induced John to sollicit that accommodation.[6] Many learned writers of that time say, that the question was not then about John's heir, but about the old story the choice of a steward, and the perpetual contract we have mentioned. But be this as it will, there was no disagreement between John and his sister on either of these points, as Sir Humphrey Polisworth himself doth acknowledge. On the contrary, if John roared against Squire Geoffry, Peg tore her cap and her apron in perfect rage, and was like cat and dog with the same Squire and his gang, all the time they were in the management of John's business.

The truth of the matter was, that about the time of the great change we have mentioned, many people in both families said, 'Although we agree now, we may quarrel hereafter, and it will be a plaguey thing to come into the hands of different lawyers and attornies again, who never fail to set people by the ears for their own advantage. John and Margaret have lived so much better, since they came to employ the same lawyer, that it is a pity they should ever be in danger of parting their affairs. The lands of Bull-hall and Thistledown[7] were never intended for two farms, the same hedge and ditch surround them, and whilst they continue in one, they may be kept with half the looking after; for nobody can be half so troublesome to either family, as they have formerly been to one another.' For these, and many more reasons, an agreement[8] was thought upon; and though it went somewhat against John's stomach, yet he coaxed and flattered sister Peg till he obtained her consent, not to come to live in his house, as the learned Sir Humphrey Polisworth has erroneously related, but merely to shut up her own compting-room, dismiss her overseers, and send her clerks to John's house, to manage their affairs together with his accomptant, under the inspection of the great lawyer, as he was then called, in both families.

This agreement, however, did not please every body. The servants who attended Peg's compting-room, were angry at the loss of their vails.[9] The upper servants, as every body knows, mismanaged their part of the business[10] some how or other, and many people said, that the house looked melancholy when the windows of the counting-room just looking to the South were shut up. In short, you could hear a buzz in every corner of the house, that the whole family was undone for ever. Jack himself grew very sulky, and for the turn of a straw would have played the devil. But what will not a little time do.[11] Peg's people got gradually into better humour; Jack's zeal for the contract made with Sir Thomas, soon reconciled him to whatever was connected with it, and Peg's affairs went on so tolerably, that every body was pacified, except the few who would be pleased with nothing, unless Squire Geoffry was restored.

About the time that Sir Thomas came to the office, there was a great turmoil[12] in John's kitchin and backyard, and in Peg's garret, where indeed she harboured a parcel of curious fellows,[13] who did not mind the business of the family much, but would run you up and down stairs like lightning, sometimes get into the kitchen, the hen roost, or back yard, and snap up any thing their fingers could lay hold of. Their mistress seldom got any

rent from them, except a day's work now and then in harvest, or
the use of their children to keep the crows from the barley. But
the true secret of her liking to them was, that they were excellent fellows at a brawl, and you had as good put your head in the
fire, as meddle with their mistress when they were by. But Peg
could never get them to agree among themselves till very lately,
nor always to behave very respectfully to herself; insomuch, that
both John and she were often tempted to condemn that garret.
But things must have their course, the garret gentry[14] have sometimes done excellent service, and there is nobody John himself
likes better to see about him, when Lewis Baboon or Lord Strutt
come about cudgel-playing, which is a very common case, as the
learned Sir Humphrey has very well observed.

CHAP. I.

HOW JOHN QUARRELLED WITH LEWIS BABOON ABOUT DIVIDING THE WEST-COMMON; AND HOW INSTEAD OF GOING TO LAW, THEY CAME TO BLOWS.

We account it a great oversight in the learned Sir Humphrey
Polisworth, that he has taken little or no notice of John Bull's
land-estate, his orchards, kitchen-grounds, and cornfields, of
which he has always possessed an excellent share; but considered
him as a simple clothier and mechanic, merely because he sent
goods of this, and many other kinds to market. John got ready
money, it is true, by the sale of his goods; but the great support
of his family, and what made him be treated like a gentleman in
the neighbourhood, was the excellent manor of Bull-hall, where
John and his posterity may find capon and bacon, and beef and
mutton, without being obliged to any body, and without cring-
ing to Lord Strutt, Squire South, or Lewis Baboon, for their
custom. It is true, that the devil possessed John sometimes to that
degree, that you could not hear a word from him but about his
cloth, and his iron-work, and his pottery, and you would see him
up to the eyes in clay, or steeped, till he grew all the colours of

the rainbow, in dyer's stuff, or smoaked and roasted like a smith, or sallow and greasy like a weaver, and no gentleman could keep company with him, or any of his family, such low habits they had got behind the counter, or in the work-shop. 'Mind your customers, lads,' says John; 'Good words go far; Be civil to every body whether they buy or no;' and then he would rap out a string of proverbs, such as 'A penny saved is a penny got; Fast bind, fast find,' and so forth; in short, if it had not been for some good blood which John had still in his veins, he must have grown a mere pedling, sneaking, designing, mercenary rogue, as ever was.

There was, as we say, blood, or something else, that kept up John's spirit, so that he went abroad now and then, in as gentleman-like a way as could be wished, although Lewis Baboon used to sit sneering at him sometimes as he passed; but John minded him not a rush.

Now it happened, that John and Lewis had about the same time taken in part of the west-common,[16] and though their fields were not contiguous, they could not agree about their marches. Many meetings[17] they had to settle them, but all to no purpose, for none of them knew well what he would be at.[18] The common saying was, that Lewis wanted to get all the land in the country, and you needed only to tell John so much, in order to put him in a downright foam of rage and fury. However this be, Lewis tormented his own people enough, with making them stick in posts[19] and stakes in different parts of the common, and when John asked him what he meant, he said, They were only rubbing posts for his cows to scratch themselves, in case they strayed so far. But other people told John, that Lewis would some day or other claim every bit of that ground as his own, by virtue of those stakes, if he was not checked in time. Accordingly, John sent him some angry message about them, and Lewis in return, begged leave to present his compliments to John, and assured him, that the thing in the world he wished most, was to live in good terms with his honoured friend and neighbour John Bull. Mean time, some of John's cowherds met with a fellow or two belonging to Lewis, and after a great deal of bad language, painful to repeat, they came to blows,[20] and made a great noise, which brought John and Lewis too, to see what was the matter. John, indeed, happened to be in his barge that afternoon, on the lake to the west of his house, which he affected to call his own fish-pond, and Lewis too being on his way to the common, their barges[21] unhappily met, when John, without any more ado, took up an oar, and aimed a blow at Lewis Baboon's brains, 'You damn'd, insidious, fair-tongued villain, this is all your doing, with your stakes and your posts, and your covetousness for land, which nobody will possess under you, you damned, oppressive, squeezing rascal.' 'My dear John', says Lewis, 'what is the matter?' 'The matter, you scoundrel!' With that John aimed another blow; but their barges ran foul of one another, and he fastened on Lewis Baboon's wig, tore his bag, and threw it in the water; in short, before you could count six, there was not a hat nor a wig to be seen in the whole boats-crew, of either side. History says, that Lewis had like to have been drowned outright, and was glad to get home with his head broken in many places, and cursing John Bull, for the most rash, cholerick, blunder-headed fellow, that ever was known in the world.

CHAP. II.

WHAT SORT OF FELLOWS JOHN AND LEWIS WERE IN USE TO EMPLOY TO KEEP THEIR ORCHARDS, AND THEIR POULTRY.

History tells us many lies, if this was the first time that John and Lewis came to blows; and Sir Humphrey Polisworth may think to conceal it if he will, but many a time has Lewis, in his youth, lost his hat and his wig in scuffles with John, and as often has John come home with a broken pate, though very few people durst tell it to his wife or his mother. In short, these two had been troublesome rogues to one another time out of mind; and at the time of which we are now speaking, there was no such thing as law or justice in the whole country. If you could keep your own, it was well; if not, it did not signify complaining; two or three stout fellows at your back, a brace of pistols, or a blunderbuss, was a better title to an estate than the best conveyance in the world. Whilst you thought yourself sure of your lands, two or three fellows in the neighbourhood would be disputing who should have it; and of Lord Strutt, Lewis Baboon, Squire South, Nicholas Frog, John Bull himself, and all the gang of them, there was not one to mend another, they did not mind blowing out one another's brains one farthing; they had got honourable names for thieving, robbing, and house-breaking, such as policy, conquest, and invasion; and if you lived in their neighbourhood, they were sure to leave you nothing, unless you could handle a cutlass, or fire a blunderbuss, and kept friends with some one or other of them, who protected you for his own sake, or that he might take all you had at a more convenient time. God help the poor milk-sop that trusted to the goodness of his cause.

This made every body look about him; and John among the rest, for many a day, had as stout a family of young fellows as any in all the neighbourhood, and would not take an affront or an injury from any man. His boys were for the most part sober, peaceable fellows within doors; but if there was any noise heard over-night among the poultry in the orchard, or the workshop, it needed only the bark of a dog to bring a score of them into the court, and from every corner of John's house you could hear nothing but striving who should be out first. Every body had his cutlass, or his carabine at his bed's-head, and it is hard to say which they were most jealous of, their father's honour, or the preservation of his estate. It was the pride of John's heart in those days, to see his boys hardy and resolute, and he hated a sneaking, puny, pewling fellow, like the devil.

In this humour John lived for many a day; but many changes[22] happen which nobody looks for; people persuaded him by degrees, that if he had money enough there was nothing else worth minding. From this hopeful maxim, he even neglected sending his children to school, locked up their cudgels and cricket-batts, and would not let one of them touch a gun, for fear they should hurt themselves. He had got by heart all the stories that ever his nurse had told him, about the accidents which happen at rough play, or in handling firelocks, and would repeat them sometimes, till his wife and his mother were quite ashamed of him.

It would require the pen of a great historian to tell how this great change was brought about.[23] Some people[24] said, that John was old and began to doat; others said, that it was all owing to an old nurse[25] who lived about the house; but alas, they do not tell us how John came to be directed by old women, or what was the reason that some of John's neighbours were grown worse than even he was at this time. Lewis Baboon was grown from a spruce forward gallant, a mere priest-ridden, whore-ridden, flimsey periwig-making old fool. Lord Strutt could never be got out of his bed before eleven o'clock in the morning; and Nicholas Frog would rather have taken ready money for a farthing-candle, than see his best friend return from the grave. One stout man could have chaced a hundred of them into the sea, and yet these damned fellows contrived to be very troublesome for all that, by means of a device of which the devil himself was certainly the author. In their younger days they were all ready enough at a blow, yet as they and every body about them, had some other business besides fighting, they could not well quarrel when they were otherways engaged; but they came at last to keep people on purpose to fight, and as nobody cared what became of these fellows, they would send them out for the turn of a straw, to play the devil in all the neighbourhood; and the rest of the people at home trusting to them, became mere milk-sops and old women.

An historian of great credit affirms that this practice was grafted on that of keeping a game-keeper; and for this reason it is, that although there be many more of them in every house than are necessary to keep the game, they are nevertheless known under the title of game-keepers even unto this day. In former times, continues he, every father of a family and his children, were sportsmen more or less. It mattered not who started the game, they could all shoot without distinction; and it mattered as little what part of the house a thief attempted to break in upon, the first man he met thought himself obliged to defend the premises. But when they grew lazy, spiritless, and purse-proud, they must needs keep their game-keepers like lords,[26] and each according to his estate, got as many as he could well maintain, and those he employed not only to knock down a hare, or a partridge, now and then, for the master's table, but to them he entrusted the whole defence of his estate inclosed and common, barn-yards, orchards, and kitchin-grounds, and it was thought presumption in any body else to do any thing besides running away when any body attempted to disturb the house. Lewis Baboon would have kept you forty or fifty at a time,[27] and this when nobody was meddling with him, as he said, to guard his poultry, and attend him to church.

These fellows did nothing from morning to night, but first turn upon one heel, and then upon another, put a gun sometimes to their hip, sometimes to their nose, sometimes to their shoulder; and, in short, played so many antic tricks with a musket, that few or none of them could remember or distinguish its real use. But they bilked their landlords, cursed, swore, and bullied, wherever they went, and in many houses where such fellows were kept, nobody durst say his life was his own for them.

It may be hard enough to tell how any master of a family came to keep such people about him; but the most amazing thing of all is, how John Bull, so kind a father, and so good a master, should ever think of entertaining so many of them, and trust more to their affection, than to that of his own children.

It is true, that John's heart has always misgiven him in this project; he generally keeps a dozen or so, but nobody could ever prevail on him, or Mrs Bull, to tell how long they were to keep them; and every Saturday night when he pays off his workmen, he always says, 'Gentlemen, whereas it goes against my conscience, to keep some damned rascals perpetually about my house, you are to remain only for next week, and no longer'; but still he keeps them on in this manner from one week to another, for which he has many salvos. 'In the first place', says John, 'I don't take any body but my own tenants's sons, or now and then an idle fellow from my own farm, and I have always some of my own boys who keep them company; so that they always behave very respectfully to me, and have often taken my part, when such fellows as Nicholas Frog keeps would have cut my throat. 'Secondly', says John, 'I only keep them as long as Squire Geoffrey and his abettors are like to be troublesome, which I hope will not be long.' But many of John's enemies said, that there was a better reason than all these put together, viz. that he was afraid to fire a gun himself, and was frightened out of his senses when he had not some of his bullies by him.

Whether this was the cause, or the effect of his keeping those fellows, it must be owned that John Bull, who used to be a bold hearty fellow, always master in his own house, and afraid of nothing, began to sneak about the doors, and would start at his own shadow; and when there was any noise in the orchard, or poultry-yard, he would scour up to the garret, and leave the game-keepers and the thieves to do what they pleased with his effects, shutting his eyes, and stopping his ears, that he might not see or hear any shooting of guns, of which in truth he was become marvelously afraid.[28] Lewis Baboon had no more ado, but to give out that he was going to pay a civil visit to John, in order to put the whole house in a pannic; and this word *pannic*[29] was grown so familiar with John, that he had it always ready as an excuse for running away upon the slightest occasion.

CHAP. III.

HOW JOHN *GOT A TERRIBLE FRIGHT IN HIS OWN HOUSE OF BULL-HALL.*

It was not always without cause, that John Bull disliked the visits of Lewis Baboon; he knew what fine sport that rogue might have made for himself in such a house; and that besides cuckoldom, many other misfortunes might have befallen the landlord. But history, with all her gravity, will scarcely make posterity believe, how much John was afraid of his own sister Margaret's garret lodgers. Once upon a time, two or three of them being seduced by some outlandish person, who stiled himself young Mr Geoffrey,[30] got down stairs, ran into Margaret's dining room and drawing-room, overset the china, drank the cream, and having found one of John's game-keepers[31] teaching the maids to coddle apples in the back-kitchen, gave him a slap in the chops, and poured the scalding water on him. From thence they proceeded as they thought proper; and though Margaret threw her poker[32] at them as they passed, with an air of great bitterness and vexation, yet John took it in his head that it was all her doing, and sent her word to keep them at home, otherwise he would set fire to her house: but just as he was talking in this strain, and abusing his poor sister as a treacherous vixin, who might have kept better order in her house if she pleased, he was silenced at once with a knock on the pate;[33] and without staying to see what was the matter, ran up to the leads, called out to his game-keepers, who were gone nobody knows where, then to Nicholas Frog, Rousterdivel, and all the damned names you can think of, to come to the assistance of John Bull, whose throat was just going to be cut in his own house.

Mean time, MacLurchar, for this was the ringleader in all this mischief, continued to do what he pleased. Whenever he met any of John's fellows, he asked, 'What trade are you?' And if they were weavers, he made them furnish what cloth he wanted; threatening to rip up their guts. In like manner, if they were brewers, tanners, cooks, scullions, or malsters, each in his way had something good for MacLurchar, and the fellow had learned not to be afraid, although there were three hundred of them together.

This fray, however, did not last long; MacLurchar was tired, and went away home to his garret, and John, who had been more afraid than hurt, came down stairs, and when he saw that the foe was actually gone, called out to set fire to Peg's house, to burn her, and all her vermin; for, says he, we shall never get any peace for them. Mean time, the game-keeper[34] took heart at last, went up to the garret, and gave MacLurchar a stunning blow in the guts,[35] just as he was stripping to go to bed, and dragged him down to the court, where John was in a little prevailed on to come and see the object of his terror, with his hands tied behind his back. Then, indeed, he began to be ashamed of his own behaviour, and abused all his people for letting him be so much afraid; he scolded the very scullions for letting the bacon be carried off by so paultry a fellow as MacLurchar.[36] In short, he and everybody else threw the blame upon his neighbour, but all agreed in cursing and sinking sister Peg, to the deepest pit of hell.

It was hard to say what the poor woman had done to deserve all this treatment; but some people set to work with here merely because it was the fashion, and others found their account in it, some in one way, some in another. As for the game-keeper, it was not very difficult to see his motive; he had never beat any body before in all his life, and wanted now to magnify his feats as much as he could, and accordingly said, that few people knew the amount of what he had done; that if he had not fought with

sister Margaret's people one and all, he was no true man; that he
totally subdued them, and knew of nobody to compare himself
to, but the ancient conquerors.[37] That if any body said, that the
whole of Margaret's people was not against him, he was a
scoundrel, and a rascal, and not to be trusted.

After this, who and who were to be trusted became the great
question in John's house. There was no pretending to any thing
without being able to talk about trusting; and some people
would scarcely let John Bull trust himself. As for poor Peg, he
was the finest fellow that spoke the most ill of her. Even some
of her own children who took care of nobody but themselves all
the time that MacLurchar was stirring, came abroad now to
confess with regret, that their mother was a sad vixin; that she
had given MacLurchar a dram of cherry-brandy, before he set
out upon that damned unnatural diabolical hell-fire scamper;
that for their parts it was true, they had the misfortune to be
born in her house, some people said of her own proper person,
but few people know who their real parents are: this, however,
they knew, that they had left her very young, and never liked
her company. When one had made such a speech as this, another
endeavoured still to improve upon it; and if one gave his mother
two, three, or more abusive epithets, the next did not fail to give
five or six. At last one great dolt of a fellow, called Bumbo, made
a shift to get a round dozen of them on his finger ends, with
which he never failed to entertain John Bull as often as he met
him.

The sequel of all this spite to their mother, was a great deal
of kindness to John Bull. 'Leave matters to us', said they, 'we
shall take care that so worthy a man shall not be imposed upon;
you should always have some of us about your own person, and
give us some decent employment, that no body may suspect the
design of our being here; we shall take care to place people[38] in
that unnatural sister's house, so that not a whisper shall be
uttered among her gossips, but you shall hear of it'; and these
speeches they commonly concluded, with a *beware of counter-
feits*. John upon all this looked like a perfect oaff: he thought
MacLurchar's knife was at his throat every moment; and these
favourable dispositions they took care to improve. One time he
was told that a cousin of MacLurchar's had come in secretly at
Peg's garret window; at another time, that MacLurchar himself

had bought a pair of new shoes; at another time, that his sister Margaret had laughed at him, when she heard that he went up to the leads; and all this, besides being asked regularly every morning, what would become of him, if he had not some trusty friends to stand between him and that unnatural sister. In short, John was put from his sleep and his appetite; he stared and stammered in his speech; you could not hear a word of common sense from him; and to have spoken a word of common sense, would have disgraced you with him for ever.

History says, however, that John did not continue very long in this humour; and, indeed, it must be owned, that it was for once a good thing to be of a changeable temper: it would have been the devil indeed, to have continued for ever in the hands of spies and informers, perpetually talking of the miseries of human life; and the truth is, that there was nothing in the world more repugnant to his ordinary temper; so that though he could not all at once return to a perfect cordiality with his sister, yet he listened to people who advised him to take gentle methods with her. He accordingly, let even MacLurchar himself off, with little more than an obligation to put on his breeches[39] every morning before he came down stairs among the ladies; and sent a civil message to his sister, to ask her how she did, and to propose taking a lease of her garret, and said that he would pay her any rent she chose to put upon it. Many odd projects, indeed, were put in his head at this time; such as to turn that garret into a stable and coach-house; to make sister Peg lodge her coals in it, brew her ale, and wash her linen; in short, to make MacLurchar himself, besides putting on his breeches, carry up earth, and plant cabbages and turnips upon the leads. It is true, that nothing of all this has been done; but it is not John's fault, he was at some expense about it, and meant all for the best.

CHAP. IV.

HOW JOHN'S *AFFAIRS HAD LIKE TO HAVE GONE TO THE DEVIL.*

We know how difficult a thing it is to write history. Whenever the reader meets with any thing that exceeds his own pitch, he presently attacks the credit of the historian; and we shall now be asked how came John Bull, who was such a coward in his own house, to be so very rash, as we have said, in that scuffle with Lewis Baboon. The fact is, that John never was slow at getting into a quarrel; he was choleric beyond measure; and as for mischief out of doors, there was nobody readier. He had a parcel of watermen who feared neither man nor devil, and when he was in his barge, either on the east or the west lake, it was but a word and a blow with him; he never was afraid to meet with Lewis Baboon there, nor any where else, except at home. When you proposed to John, to go over to Lewis's own house, and break his bones for him, he thought nothing more easy; but alas, if Lewis talked of coming to him, matters went no better than we have said.

You will easily believe, that after that scuffle in the barge, Lewis Baboon must be in a very great passion. Accordingly, he cursed and swore like twenty dragoons, that he would speedily see John in his own house, and show him in the face of Mrs Bull herself, what sort of a man he had affronted: this was sooner said than done. But in the mean time, nobody could tell what was become of John, and all his watermen; whilst Lewis Baboon went vapouring about every where, and did what he pleased. He drove John's cattle out of Cracket-Island,⁴⁰ and took possession of it; although John used to think that nobody could ever dispute islands with him, so ready was he with his barge to relieve them: but the truth upon this occasion was, that John had got into one of these pannics we have mentioned, had applied to Nicholas Frog to no purpose, and actually brought over Rousterdivel, to protect him. But the whole neighbourhood laughed at him, when they saw that Lewis Baboon had no more to do than to talk of going over to John, in order to do what he pleased every where else; and John got into one of the greatest passions that ever he was in in his life. All the historians of that time, ring with the amazing noise which he made about that same Cracket-Island. He swaggered and stared, and roared and swore, that John Bull of Bull-Hall was abused and cheated by his clerks, his watermen, his overseers, and every soul about him. When he saw Rousterdivel, he called to his people to turn out that fellow; asked, what the devil had brought him to his house; would not give him a bit of victuals, and threatened to go to law with him about a handkerchief: and in short, obliged the poor fellow to go away, very much puzzled to make out what sort of a man this same Mr Bull must be.

Upon this occasion, John made such a noise, that he wakened Mrs Bull, and brought her down yawning to the parlour, and rubbing her eyes, after one of those drousy fits, to which she had been lately subject. He had already, to her no small mortification, chaced away two or three of her favourite servants, who used to put her to bed every night, and among the rest his own nurse,[41] who was grown of late a great person in all Mrs Bull's junketings and private parties; and indeed, for some time, pretended to manage John himself as she thought proper. To do this nurse justice, there were few people had a better hand at a sack-posset; and though she had no aversion to a glass of liquor in a fair way, yet she never tasted what came through her hands in the way of making cawdle, whey, or panada for the children: we never heard any thing amiss of her, save that she would take the children's halfpence from them to keep, and therewith make up little sums, which she lent to the servant maids at interest, when they wanted to buy ribbons, or other trinkets. But the love of money may be forgiven in old age,[42] as also that meddling disposition which servants usually acquire when they have been long about a house. The truth is, that nothing could be more ridiculous than to hear this old woman put in her word upon all occasions. There was nothing in which she did not think herself a perfect oracle; she talked to John not only about his markets and his bargains, and all his dealings with his neighbours, about the choice of schools and masters for his children; game-keepers, huntsmen, whippers-in; but, in short, about his drunken quarrels, boxing matches, cudgel play, and quarter staff. She would govern every part of his house for him, and no servant durst go with a message from his master, without first asking her, if she had any commands.

Hubble-bubble,[43] and this nurse, had gone hand in hand for many a day; but alas! the loss of Cracket-Island fell heavy upon them both at last. Bawd, whore and rogue,[44] were the best names they could get from John upon that occasion, and Hubble-bubble got out of his way as fast[45] as he could scour, but the nurse broke a cawdle-cup which she had in her hand, and bid him go find another to make slops for himself and his children.

John was greatly helped into this fine humour by one Jowler, for whom he had a great regard at this time. Most historians agree, that the name of Jowler was only a nick-name, which this fellow had got from the boys at school, on account of some odd conceit of a resemblance between him and a hound of that name in John's pack. They say, moreover, that most of the boys had the name of some dog or other given them, and that they used to make one of themselves the hare, and so hunt him with a mighty noise, in imitation of John's pack. As to the dog Jowler, his resemblance to the person we are now speaking of, has procured him a place in the records of history. There we are told, that this dog had a very loud tongue, and that if he could not lead the whole pack, he never failed, at least, to carry off five or six couple, sometimes on a right, sometimes on a wrong scent; that he thereby so often spoilt the sport, that the huntsman was downright crazy with rage, and often threatened to turn Jowler out of the kennel, and sometimes actually tied him up at home; but then he made such a noise, that Mrs Bull could get no sleep for him in a morning; and the huntsman was as often obliged to leave Mango's tomb and plaister in the kennel, whilst Jowler was suffered to lead the pack. Then John had excellent sport, and the huntsman no great cause to complain; for Jowler was tractable enough, and a crack of the whip would make him leave the pursuit of the stag, for that of a pole-cat, or a rabbit, and this not absolutely for want of nose, but for fear of being turned down among the babblers again.

Although we account it below the dignity of history, to adopt, or retail nick-names, yet we think ourselves obliged in this case, to retain a name which has come down to us on the great tide of writers,[46] which waft and carry the transactions of that age. To return, therefore, from this digression; Jowler no sooner observed the humour which John was in, than he chimed in directly; he told him that his family had never been so much disgraced

before; that the scandalous loss of Cracket-Island was more owing
to his overseer, than to the waterman who was sent[47] to look
after it; that it was ignominious for John Bull, with a house full
of fine young fellows, to need the protection of so sorry a fellow
as Rousterdivel; that if he did not look about him, he would soon
become the jest of all the neighbourhood, and lose all the ground
which he had upon the common, or any where else. To approve
of a man's advice in one thing, and trust him with every thing,
were inseparable with John; accordingly, he put all his affairs
directly into Jowler's hands,[48] and for the first fortnight neither
Sir Thomas, nor any body else, durst controul him in any thing.

CHAP. V.

HOW JOHN CONSULTED WITH HIS FRIENDS ABOUT THE METHOD OF RETRIEVING HIS AFFAIRS.

John was a great person for collecting his friends together to
have their advice, but for the most part he did just what he
pleased for all that; and he had always some point or other in his
head, in which it was in vain to contradict him. This was the
case now about the malversations of his servants, and though
there were many people disposed to soften him, not a mortal
durst put in a word. In the height of his passion he abused
every thing that had been done,[49] right or wrong, for many
years before. They had neglected his new farm upon the common, and sent his horses, his ploughs and carts, to labour Sir
Thomas's land[50] in the east country; they had run him in debt
over head and ears, pawned his plate, and mortgaged his estate;
they had made his wife, who used to be a notable woman, a mere
sot, with ale, brandy, and slops. The nurse had even spoilt his
own stomach with nasty mawkish warm drinks, and over-
heating his ale. With all this in his head, whenever he went to
any of the neighbouring towns, he instantly repaired to the
coffee-house,[51] and poured all forth to the first person he met.
All the world admired the vigour of his spirit, and the honesty

of his intentions, even when he carried matters too far; and we all know, that if the father of such a family does not make a noise sometimes, affairs will be managed but so so.

About this time of which we are now speaking, John had a circle about him wherever he went, and talked of his affairs from morning to night. He testified a particular aversion to the employing of Rousterdivel any more, swore that he himself never would cross the lake upon any body's errands, and that if any body came over to meddle with him, he would show them that he could defend himself. In all which, Jowler encouraged him strongly, and repeated every word John could say, in a much higher tone than himself; and next to the point of getting fixed in the management of the business, seemed to have nothing more at heart, than to break off all idle connections, to keep John at home, and put a gun in his own hands, to avoid the disgrace of running to other people for protection on every trifling alarm. Whatever might be done afterwards, Jowler knew this was no time to baulk John in any of his fancies; and accordingly, he assisted in all his consultations, and nobody so loud as he.

One day, when John's tongue was running on God knows where, he was asked by some of his friends what he intended to do. 'Do you intend', said they, 'to ask Lewis Baboon's pardon for striking him in the manner you did, or do you persist in the design of giving him gentlemany satisfaction?' 'I tell you what', says John, 'if Lewis Baboon had a thousand Cracket-Islands of mine, and that he would give me them all for asking his pardon, I would not do it. He is a vile, over-reaching, undermining, treacherous rogue, and there never will be any peace in the neighbourhood, as long as that fair-tongued rascal is out of his grave. Let him come out in his barge again, and I shall meet him; but I know the rascal, he has perpetually some bad design in his head, and when he is found out, he will bow and scrape, and make compliments; but he does not lay it aside for all that, he only waits for a time to put it in execution, not in a fair gentlemany way, but behind your back, or when you are asleep, or indisposed: but I will dress his jacket for him, if I find him put his nose upon the lake again'.

'But only suppose then', said they, 'that he should slip over in the night, as he has often threatened, with a parcel of his game keepers, and take possession of your parlour and bedchamber, which are worth more than Cracket-Island to him, do you think, he will give you time to send for Rousterdivel, as you used to do?'

'All the fires of Sodom and Gomorrah seize me,' says John, 'if ever I send for Rousterdivel with his great tobacco-pipe, his sour crout, and his damned lingo, that nobody can understand. Oddsblood, an't I as good a man as Rousterdivel or Lewis Baboon? Though I have not so many game-keepers, yet I have as good clean-made fellows about my farm as he; and if my own children will let me be insulted, it is time that John Bull was gone the way of all flesh.'

'But what can your children do for you', said they, 'when your wife, and your nurse, and your steward, will not let one of them touch a gun or a cutlass, and think there is no safety but in the dark cellar, or the coal-hole, when there is any disturbance in the yard?'

'Well', says John, 'I shall tell them another tale; my boys shall learn to defend me as they used to do. I have seen the time when the stoutest of them all durst not meddle with me, and that time shall return again, if I can get arms enough to furnish my hall, as I always had it, till now.'

CHAP. VI.

HOW THE NURSE DREAMT THAT JOHN BULL HAD BANISHED ALL THE WEAVERS.

We may believe that after so busy a day, as we have been describing, the Nurse was not likely to get a very good night's rest; starting, tumbling and tossing she had in abundance, but very little sound sleep. She could not shut an eye, but presently she dreamt[52] of some mischief or other. One time she thought the pan boiled over in the fire; at another time, that the cat's paw was in the custard; and finally, about three o'clock in the morning, she dreamt that John Bull had banished all the weavers from his house; she saw the beams, the tradles, the shuttles, the pirns, all tumbled in a heap into a great black boat; she saw all the weavers posting to embark. When she would have seized a piece of broad-cloth, behold it was a great iron cannon! When she put out her hand to save a pirn, lo, it perked up in her face in the make of a pistol! Terror and amazement awakened her; she forgot her resolution never to talk any more to John Bull about his affairs, and thought herself now called upon by heaven, to interpose in behalf of him and his children.

Accordingly, she lost no time in the morning, but went straight to the parlour, where she found John as busy as ever, talking about the orders he was to give in his house: and having told him her dream, earnestly beseeched him to tell her, whether he had any such intention, with relation to the weavers; for she thought that a person, who had ceased to be guided by her, would stick at nothing.

'The woman is crazy', says John: 'I am only thinking how I may best secure the peace and welfare of my family, and how to keep off rogues; and you ask me, if I am to banish my weavers? I'll defend my weavers to the last drop of my blood; they shall fare no worse than I do; late or early, if they are molested, I shall be with them, and I know that they will stand by me against all the world.'

'What better protection can you desire for yourself or them', says the nurse, 'than your own game-keeper, or Rousterdivel? It would do one good to see, how that fine tall fellow will stop and turn, and do what he is bid.'

'A plague take the woman', says John, 'with her Rousterdivel; do you think that I am a coward, a scoundrel, a beast, a block-head, a milk-sop, that I must always run for protection to other people? I tell you again, that I am able to defend myself, and that I have people enow[53] about my house to stand by me.'

'And how do you propose that they should stand by you?' says the nurse: 'When Lewis sends over his game-keepers, with their guns and their sabres, who will stand by you then?'

'Odso', says John, 'cannot my people have guns and sabres as well as they?'

'Alas! then', says the nurse, 'my dream is read. You will not have a weaver in your house in three days, if you go on at that rate: who do you think will sit quietly on a loom, with guns and pistols pointing at them in every corner, and that boy George putting crackers in the candles, and firing his pistols at sparrows, and shooting the neighbours's cats when they come about the hedges? See who can settle to work for you, if they are in perpetual danger of having their eyes blown out with squibs, serpents and rackets? Do you think a tradesman can do any good if he is scared at that rate?'

'Scared!' says John, 'you don't think that a weaver will be scared when he turns game-keeper, and I have none better on my grounds. If any of my people are afraid of a gun, so much the more shame to them and to me; it is the very thing I want to correct, by using them a little to what may be necessary for their own defence and mine.'

'Worse and worse', says the nurse: 'if you use them to guns, you'll never get them to work a jot; and banishing the trade is worse than banishing the men.'

'A tenfold madness has seized your pericranium', says John; 'do you think that nobody can make broad cloth but cowards; or that a fellow won't work, because he knows he can defend the fruits of his labour? You have no objection to the taking as many of my tradesmen as you can get, to make game-keepers of them; and because they work none, you imagine that every fellow who takes a firelock in his hand to defend himself and me, is to be idle too. Don't the game-keepers themselves work when they are allowed, and are paid for it? have not I known them give money to their overseers, for leave to work at their own trades? and many a good penny has been got in that way. As my people are useful to me, and to themselves, I intend that they shall work in safety, and that nobody shall insult an honest tradesman of mine, whilst they and I have breath in our bodies. Do what you will, you shall never get me disgraced as you have done, with your idle jaw and nonsensical trash.'

'Bless me', says the nurse, 'what a wild project you have got in your head! You'll tell me you want to defend your house and your estate; but to what purpose keep your estate, if you cannot find time, so much as to eat a bit of warm victuals; hurried late and early, banged, soused and drenched in all weathers, and this for fear that Lewis Baboon should turn you out of your possessions; and what matter who has your possessions, if you cannot sit down to enjoy them? *Et propter vitam vivendi perdere causas*.'

'Hey-day', says John, 'your humble servant, Latin! I remember you of old.[54] But goody', says he, 'I knew you lived among the boys; but don't think to palm upon me as a commendation of eating and drinking and cowardice, what the old boy for whom I have so often been whipped, damn him, has said against a fellow who would forfeit his honour to preserve his life.'

'Well then', says the nurse, 'see how you can keep your bargain with Sir Thomas. What will he say, when he sees your house swarming with pistols and carabines, and cutlasses? you know that he does not chuse to trust any body in this house with gun-powder, except the game-keeper.'

'Blood-and-wounds', says John, 'you are more mindful of Sir Thomas than you are of me. I have heard nothing from you these twenty years, but Sir Thomas does not like this, and Sir Thomas does not like that. I was advised to take Sir Thomas into the management of my affairs, because Squire Geoffrey endeavoured to get a game-keeper of his own, and do what he pleased about my house. And now you tell me, that Sir Thomas and the game-keeper are the only people to be trusted. Those gentlemen, it seems, will trust nobody else, and who the devil will trust them? I never knew any of those suspicious people, that was much to be trusted himself. Ill doers are ill dreaders, as my sister Peg says. Odso, if Sir Thomas does not think himself safe in my parlour with me and my children, he must know of something worse than I thought of. Who was it that brought him about the house? Have not I done all that lay in my power for him? And now you and he won't let me defend myself, because he won't trust me. I love Sir Thomas; I mean, that he shall have the disposal of all the arms about my house, and he shall find that I am his friend, when Hubble-bubble and you are in your graves, and all the nonsense you are perpetually putting in his head and mine, is not worth a curse.'

CHAP. VII.

WHAT HAPPENED AFTER THIS CONVERSATION WITH THE NURSE.

Who was listening to all this discourse, but the very boy George himself, whom the nurse was so much afraid of? This youngster, instead of loitering about the kitchen or the nursery, flattering the cook-maid, or the nurse, for slops and tit-bits between meals, was perpetually rambling about in quest of some diversion without doors. He had procured a pistol and a gun, and powder and shot, all which he hid in the hay-stack, or in crannies of the barn wall. You would think that he minded nothing but climbing walls, and scrambling over hedges; but no sooner did he see two or more people serious about any thing, than he forgot all his play, came to listen, as he did to this conversation between John and his nurse, and gave such attention, that there were few articles relating to the family, of which he had not an excellent notion; and could see the folly and ridicule of people, who thought themselves over wise, as well as another: he was a perfect plague to the nurse, who hated a joke,[55] and was often put downright mad with his dry wipes and arch sayings. He no sooner heard John talk in the peremptory manner above related, than he ran away to Mrs Bull as fast as his legs could carry him, and told her all that her husband had said, and a great deal more of his own, without mincing the matter in the least, by which he convinced her that John was not then in an humour to be crossed, and that whether she liked the project or no, it was best to put a good face upon the matter.

Every body knows that John had devolved great part of his business upon Mrs Bull; no tradesman's bill could be paid without her authority, nor any receipts granted to any of John's tenants. In short, neither John himself, nor Sir Thomas, durst go to a fair or a market, till they knew whether she would stand to their bargains. This had often been very troublesome to Sir Thomas, and till he found out the way of managing her by means of Hubble-bubble, and the like persons, he was obliged to proceed with great caution, and for the most part to stay at home, when he would fain have been a gadding.

John had been so oft married, that it may be said with safety, that no man in the world ever had more experience in matrimony. He had tasted at times both the sweet and the bitter; but it was a maxim of his, that any wife was better than none; and accordingly, no sooner one wife died, than he instantly married another. He never liked a woman the worse for having a spice of the vixen; it pleased him to hear the clack of a woman's tongue; and the truth is, that in a family like his, it was no good sign when the mistress was not heard of both late and early. His present wife had got herself a tolerable name in the neighbourhood, as a quiet, discreet, good sort of a woman; and John, accordingly, sometimes almost forgot that she was in the family. She never let him have any of those disputes with Sir Thomas about settling the accounts, with which John had used to be delighted; but commonly passed them in the lump, saying, that every article was just what she would have thought of herself, for the good of the family. With all this good understanding with Sir Thomas, it was suspected that she had not all the respect for her husband that she should have had; and the more that she never scrupled to talk over all the arts which she had practised in the courtship, and to tell, how many a pot and penny it had cost her, to get a good word with his servants, thereby to secure John to herself, when he might have had his choice of all the country; and then she would talk of her pin-money, and little perquisites, out of which, she was perpetually endeavouring to make up some little stock for herself. The nurse and Hubble-bubble humoured her in all this way of talking, and said, to be sure, nobody would marry such an old fellow as John Bull, except with a view to get something by him. By this, and such like discourse, they had got a great deal to say with her, and could have easily persuaded her at this time to put off the project of giving out the guns, if they durst have ventured to cross John in a thing he was so much bent upon. The boy George assured Mrs Bull, that John must have at least fifty or sixty at a time, and all that the nurse could venture upon, was to make her abate one half; with which solacing herself in the mean time, she let an order be signed for the rest.

It is hard to say, what made Hubble-bubble and the nurse so averse to this scheme. As for Hubble-bubble it is probable, as most historians agree, that he did not know very well himself. But the nurse, who was no fool, most people thought, must have some other reasons besides her dream. However this be, we shall relate facts as they occur in the course of our history.

CONCERNING SISTER PEG.

When the accounts were brought to sister Peg of all those fine doings in John's house; how Jowler was entrusted with every thing, and was driving it away like Jehu;[56] and how John had brought all his arms from the cellar, and was determined to fight with Lewis Baboon himself; and how John's hall was stuck round, as it used to be, with guns, pikes, bayonets and cutlasses, mixed, as report was, with stags branches, fox skins, and solitairs taken from Lewis in his youth; Peg expected a message every minute to desire she would garnish her hall in the same manner, and get ready the few young men she had left in her house to oppose Lewis, in case he should attempt to break in that way. But many a day passed without any tidings; and what was most surprizing of all was, that with all this lady's wonted spleen, and acrimony when she was vexed, there was scarcely a discontented word heard from her on the occasion. One morning, indeed, at breakfast, she said, that she could not blame her brother, but that she could not well understand, what Mrs Bull meant by putting such a slight upon her, or how it came to pass that her own clerks, whom she sent to the office, and who had nothing else to do but to mind her affairs, never let her hear a word of the matter.

This was almost all that she said, for a great while, and that with so little appearance of concern, that few historians have taken any notice of it. People who thought of former times, expected bad humour enough from her on this occasion; but the fact was, that this lady was greatly changed in her manners and deportment. From being jealous, captious, and ready to quarrel about a straw, she was grown in a very little time, a quiet easy-tempered, good-conditioned body, as could be wished, and this made some people think that the girl might have been always easy enough to live with, if people had not played tricks on purpose to vex her, which indeed was so often the case, that you would have thought her in a perpetual passion; and she was, by the habit of continual fretting, so much on the catch, that she thought herself affronted often, when no such thing was meant.

In those days her servants had better lose their ears, than slight her in the manner they now did, and they commonly stood as much in awe of her, as the servants in John's, or any other house could do of their master and mistress. But it was a changed world now. Her elder boys and upper servants passed most of their time out of the house, and sent any orders they pleased, about the kitchen, the cellar, or the farm; and those who stayed at home, and did the work of the family, forgot the way to complain.

Whilst John's house perpetually rung with the marrow-bones and cleavers, or cat-calls and groans either in honour or contempt of the upper-servants, according to their behaviour; insomuch, that Mrs Bull's own woman durst not give herself any saucy airs; in Peg's house all was hush, the good and the bad were used almost alike; and as to the business of the office, it was out of sight out of mind with Peg; she sent her clerks to wait upon Mrs Bull, and although she was at no pains to send people that would not require looking after, yet she never inquired any more about the matter. Accordingly, they not only neglected her concerns, but often got bits of the best, for abusing her to the nurse and the game-keeper, and others of Mrs Bull's gossips; and few or none of them thought of any thing, but how to get a share to themselves of what was going about Mr Bull's house. She had even the mortification to see some of the worst of them come home,[57] from John's counting-room, with directions to keep the keys of her cellar and pantry, and deal out the victuals to her children; in doing which, they had a wonderful jargon, which nobody could understand, but which had a strange effect in benumning and stupifying all their hearers. They talked perpetually of the *people above*, the *great folks*, or *the people in power*; and now and then would whisper Peg herself, that if she kept her temper, the *people above* might possibly make her a present of a hood, or a tippet, or a new petticoat, at a proper time; and though she did not know, who the devil these people above were, she was perpetually gulled with this sort of talk. Those who pretend to understand these matters, say, that the people above were such as had the naming of John Bull's servants, and that they contrived new offices, and a variety of perquisites and vails, on purpose to allure people, who were willing to sell their souls to hell, and cheat their own father and mother.

CHAP. IX.

HOW LEWIS BABOON *WAS BELABOURED AND DRUBBED; AND HOW* JOWLER *BEHAVED.*

What we have already set forth, was the real state of sister Margaret's affairs, when her brother took that sturdy resolution for himself, but left her out. His, indeed, was the best part of the family, and it was well that matters were carried so far. John was likely some time or other to go all lengths for his sister, as well as for himself; and it was the fashion at this time to say, that the great Jowler would never stop, till every good work was accomplished; but historians do not mention any great things that he did in the matter. It appears, indeed, that this fellow did set himself in earnest to touzle Lewis Baboon, and so beset the lake and the common, that Lewis could no where appear, without getting a knock on the pate with an oar, or a punch in the guts with a hand-hoe, and sometimes had musket-bullets whistling about his ears so thick, that he ran as if all the devils in hell were let loose at his heels.

In short, Jowler went on helter-skelter; and as long as John and his wife were in the humour of paying his bills, he hired all the poachers, game-keepers, and whippers-in in the country, and did not care a farthing for a fellow, unless he could send him off the country, to some mischief or other. For this reason he made John get as many gamekeepers as possible, but never a word of arming his own children.[58] He made up matters again with Rousterdivel,[59] gave him all he asked, and encouraged him to play the devil in the house of Squire South, John's old friend. He sent more people to look after Sir Thomas's farm, than ever were there before in this world. He brought John in bills of expence laid out in the East country, so extravagant, and consisting of so many articles, that you would have thought all the taylors and apothecaries in the country, had been concerned in making them up. But Jowler minded nothing of all this; as long as John was in the humour, he went on, and bullied and roared, and spent his money, as if the master's salvation depended on the noise which his man Jowler should make in the neighbourhood; and there was nothing to stop him, for peoples tongues were tied up, some by one thing, some by another; and well did he know how to hold one tongue, that used to be the loudest of all on the like occasions.[60]

There was, however, seldom a day but John had the news of some mischance befalling his foe Lewis, and then he had the marrow-bones and cleavers at his door, and his house rung with dancing and hornpipes, jigs, and country bumkins. It was in vain to tell him that these things would not avail his family a sixpence after all was over, and that he had forgot the fine resolutions he had taken, about the defence of his own house at home, the clearing up of his old arms, and sending his children to the fencing-school.

Jowler kept him perpetually drunk, in order to get his money to spend;[61] there was seldom a night, but he made him drink twelve bumpers, and dance three hornpipes; so that John frequently exposed himself to the neighbourhood, and in his cups talked no less than of taking the half of Lewis Baboon's estate to himself.

In all this hurry-scurry, the nurse and Hubble-bubble were laughing in their sleeves; they saw their own game played to better purpose, than ever they durst venture to play it. Sir Thomas and they got the fingering of more money than ever they had seen before in their lives, and they might lay it out where they pleased, so they let Jowler have the honour of the treat: whilst in the mean time they saw no necessity of taking the arms out of the cellar, and they hoped, that John would soon forget all that he ever said upon the subject. And so, perhaps, he would, till Lewis Baboon chose to put him in mind of it again, if it had not been for the boy George, and one or two more. But George never rested till he got his gun again, which the gamekeeper had taken from him[62] some time before; and there was no hindering of him, from getting some choice fellows together on holidays to shoot, as he had an order for it under Mrs Bull's own hand.

The nurse then thought that she would give them their bellyful; she said, that Lewis Baboon was coming, and advised Sir Thomas to call them out of their beds, at all hours of the night, to send them over hedge and ditch, from post to pillar, and never give them any rest, in hopes that they would tire of their project;

she thought that when they found there was no money to be got by the bargain, they would beg to be off. And here historians observe, that this good woman had forgotten, how much young people like fun better than money.[63] But still she made something of a bad bargain; she advised Sir Thomas never to let these people come home, because Lewis Baboon was coming, and to send away all the game-keepers to his own farm, because Lewis Baboon was not coming. In short, we can find no clear account of Lewis Baboon's real intention, in any historian of that age, much less collect any opinion about it from the conduct of John Bull's advisers at this time.

CHAP. X.

HOW SISTER PEG BEGAN TO LOOK ABOUT HER; AND HOW SHE WROTE A LETTER TO HER BROTHER JOHN.

Many were the freaks which John had taken in his head at different times: he once thought of turning lawyer, as every body knows; but he now despised that and every other profession, and would be nothing less than a duke or a lord.[64] He thought that he only wanted a suitable estate to maintain his dignity, and encouraged every scheme that was laid before him for acquiring it. He had, accordingly, twenty proposals brought him every day in writing by Jowler, all entitled, 'Speedy and easy methods of acquiring a great land estate, humbly addressed to John Bull, Esq;' Islands were to be seized here and there by main force; the whole common was to be inclosed, without enquiring who had a right there; plantations were to be cut down, and sent to market; farms were to be let to tenants that John could confide in, and every door was to be chalked with John Bull's name in great letters.

'Why should not I', says he, 'have a great estate, as well as another? Every body knows, that Lewis did not come honestly by all he has, yet the rogue is never the worse esteemed in the neighbourhood.'

76

Whilst John's head was busied with these hopeful projects, the news came that Lewis Baboon was coming in earnest. John looked like a person just awake from his first sleep, and made some motions towards the back-door, before he recollected that he had some guns ready in the hall, and that he and his people must be affronted for ever, if they did not pluck up their spirits. He saw a good many of his people ready to stand by him, and the blood returned to his face; the game-keepers were all brought into the yard; and the nurse herself was then glad to see as many of John's people in arms as possible; the watermen were sent out in the barge to meet Lewis Baboon; and John, in short, passed the night, as easily as could be expected of a man in his situation.

It is an old saying, Every man for himself, and God for us all. John in his hurry, barricading his doors, and posting his people, forgot his sister Margaret altogether. There was, indeed, a game-keeper lodged in her house, but this poor fellow could scarcely pretend to secure one door, and Lewis had twenty methods of coming into her house, where there was neither lock nor latch, nor a single pistol to resist any body, that should attempt to force his way; and the worst on't was, that Lewis had sent a sculler,[65] with some of his game-keepers boys, to take advantage of this situation. What could a poor woman do? the maids and the children screamed in every corner of the house, and Jowler sent a gun to MacLurchar, as if Peg's garret was the only place exposed, and left her pantry and her cellar to take care of themselves.

Many people in the house were of opinion, that she should write immediately to her brother John, to represent her case, and put him in mind, that when she trusted her affairs to the management of his clerks, it was in hopes that her concerns would be equally looked after with his own. Jack, who by this time had sown his wild oats, and was grown an orderly conversable fellow[66] as you would desire to see, was clear for writing this letter. 'From the little I have seen of this troublesome neighbourhood', says he, 'I am convinced that no family is safe from ill neighbours, and thievish servants, without the master and his children can take care of themselves. *As arrows are in the hands of a mighty man,* says the Psalmist, *so are children of the youth. Happy the man that hath his quiver full of them: they shall not be ashamed, but speak with the enemies in the gate.*[67] That is the true defence', says Jack, 'and let us have it. A game-keeper may be out of the way, but the child of the house is always by his father's side.' In short, as he was no trifler, so he was seldom idle, when there was any thing of consequence to be done, and never minded whether his opinion was asked or no. He spoke loudly on this occasion, and as he kept a regular correspondence with Sir Thomas, never failed to tell him his mind. Peg herself, who, as we have said, was rather gentle and inoffensive in her ordinary deportment, gave some signs of discontent and vexation; you could see a little fierceness return to her eye, and the affection and confidence with which she had always of late regarded her brother, perhaps, at this time helped to augment her displeasure. It is a grievous thing to be neglected by people to whom we make advances of kindness and respect: this, however, did not extort from her any injurious terms to her brother. If there was a cloud, it was readier to break upon his enemie's head than on his. The truth is, that instead of having that waspish cross disposition, which she had often discovered in her youth, she now needed some encouragement and spiriting up, to be able to defend her own. This did not hinder many people from thinking her greatly improved; she had, indeed, more bloom in her complexion, or was rather less pale than formerly, and was what you may call a tight comely woman to converse with, rather than one of your delicate beauties. But be her person what it would, it was necessary to defend her house and her children; and people told her, that if she would write to her brother, he would not hesitate a moment about putting it in her power to do so. Peg was not near so ready in taking resolutions as she used to be, when left entirely to shift for herself; and even so small a matter as writing a letter, she put off from day to day; at last, she got up one morning very early, and with the assistance of some of her children and relations, drew up a scroll[68] of the following letter, which was afterwards copied out fair, and sent by a careful person to her brother.

A copy of Margaret's *letter to her brother* John.

My dear Brother,
It was with great pleasure that I heard lately from people who frequent your house, that you had taken a resolution not to depend any longer upon Nicholas Frog or Rousterdivel for your defence; that you had collected your spirit very opportunely, and have since

found yourself fortified, by what is the real strength of every family, the affection and vigour of your own children. My heart warmed to the prospect of finding myself in the same situation, and I could have almost wished for an opportunity to see your children and mine fairly united, against some common oppressor, a case in which I hope they will always be invincible. But whatever my situation may be, I do not repine at your prosperity. Our interests, indeed, are unseparable, and I cannot be persuaded, when matters go well with you, that they can, at the long run, go ill with me or my family. This made me bear patiently with your people's neglect of me, when they ordered your family into a posture of defence; and indeed, unless it had come of yourself at that time, I was unwilling to have any matter started, which might have embarrassed you in what you was about, by furnishing, as I was told it might do, the people who were disposed to cross you, with arguments against your scheme. Those gentlemen, it seems, have a language ready prepared with respect to me, but I enter into no contentions with them. It seems that words have their weight after their meaning has ceased to be believed. It is in this way only, that I can understand, why a suspicion thrown upon me in words should be regarded, whilst your servants in my own sight, carry arms to MacLurchar, the only person almost whom you or I have reason to distrust. I do not condemn that proceeding of yours; it is an instance of your openness and good-nature, and I believe has met with a fellow, who has the heart to stand by his friends, and who, if properly directed, will fight for you and me, rather than for any body else.

But whatever my reasons were, for delaying to put you and Mrs Bull in mind of me, I cannot, in justice to my own family, delay it any longer. Your prosperity I shall always consider as my own; but there are certain distinctions, which if borne in silence by me, must, even in your own opinion, render me unworthy of the relation I bear to you. You used to call me proud. I wish I may not have erred on the other extreme. When you cease to be proud, I shall not esteem my brother the more. But whatever weaknesses I may have, how could you for a moment think of reducing me to the necessity of asking as a favour, what is the birth-right of all mankind, liberty to defend myself? I was possessed of this liberty, before I entrusted my affairs to the management of your servants; and if you and I both afterwards ceased to use it, that part of our history, perhaps, had better be past in silence. It never occurred to me, that you might perhaps resume it yourself, without offering it to me.

If a partial distribution of arms in your own family alarmed you, as it must do every man of common reason, what must I think? the only person to whom the means of self-defence are denied, whilst I

79

am surrounded on every hand, by those who carry a badge of superiority, more certain than scepters or empty pageantry. If my neighbours are at variance, whoever is uppermost, it seems, I must be at under, a poor tame drudge, unable to keep my own, or assist my friends.

I should tire you, if I was to say every thing that occurs to me on this alarming subject, and upon an occasion which would justify greater degrees of impatience than I have hitherto expressed. When I think, that the very enemy against whom your people have taken such care to secure themselves, is now hovering about my doors, where he is sure neither to find lock nor bar, nor a single musket to oppose his entry, I may well lose my patience, and wish at least to hear the cause of this difference explained.

I shall direct my own people with you, how to act upon this occasion; and I must beg the favour, that you will assist in procuring me directions how to proceed in warding off the blow, with which I am now threatened; or let me know where I am to find bread for my children, if what I have within my doors is the property of every fool, who may be disposed to take it.

I am,

with the sincerest esteem
and affection, yours, &c.

MARGARET.

This letter had a tone of impatience, perhaps, because it was the sudden burst of a sentiment, which Margaret had been at some pains to stifle. She meant, as historians affirm, only to speak of the present alarm; yet she broke into the subject at once, and then was almost ashamed to own, that she or her children were afraid of Lewis Baboon's scurvy waterman, though, to say the truth, she could then have made no defence.

CHAP. XI.

HOW THIS LETTER WAS RECEIVED BY JOHN.

Margaret certainly did her brother wrong, if she supposed that he had ever refused her the privilege of defending herself, or that he was in any degee averse, to give his consent to whatever

80

might be necessary for that purpose. The fact was, that he had forgot her altogether, and never once thought of the question, whether she should be put upon the same footing with himself in this particular.

When John Bull acted from his own temper,[69] and without reflection, he never discovered any remains of distrust or antipathy to his sister: but when any matter came to be seriously considered, and friends, as John expressed himself, were consulted, then he had, indeed, some unfavourable maxims relating to her, which he had retained from his youth, without having ever examined them since; and any ill-disposed person, putting him in mind of a bit of custard or cheese-cake, which she had snatched from him in the nursery, could have revived all his antient prejudices; and then, indeed, from his manner of talking, you would imagine that his pockets were in perpetual danger. And speaking of his sister and her family, you would imagine that he had got a nest of gypsies whom he could not dislodge from his barn, that their fingers were perfect fish-hooks or harpies's claws, perpetually sticking in his back. There were people enow who found it of use, to put him in this mood, and they were sure never to neglect it, when any of Peg's people whom they did not like, came about the house to sell trinkets, or asking for service. Then they would ask John, whether he meant to bring the itch into his family, or go to bed in perpetual fear of having his throat cut? But if any body came, who was in the use of flattering, lying, or pimping for themselves, then a lousy fellow who had been kicked out of Peg's house, was the most valuable person in the world, and John could not do too much for him.

You may believe, that if Hubble-bubble or the nurse, had been warned of a person's coming with a letter from Peg on this occasion, they would not have failed to have called, 'Stop Thief'; but by good luck the letter was delivered into their master's own hands, and they durst not for their lives say a word more on the subject at that time. John had got some bumpers[70] that afternoon; his watermen had met with Lewis Baboon's people, and he was gone abroad with Jowler, to see some boats that had been taken from Lewis, and wrecks that had been driven on shore. When he had read Peg's letter: 'Ah!' says he, 'poor sister here is mightily afraid indeed. Here is a spot of work now, Jowler. She is not so much afraid either, but she wants that her young men should be armed as well as mine.' 'Signify to her', says Jowler, 'that the greatness and importance of the affairs, in which you are now engaged, must throw all domestic details into a season of more leisure.' 'Ay, ay', says John, 'tell her we are drinking Lewis Baboon's dirge here, the fellow's joints are stiff by this time; tell her to open a new tap for her boys, let them be merry, that's all. She shall not see Lewis Baboon this twelvemonth, I warrant her. However, as to the affair of getting guns in her house, if my wife and she can agree about it, I have no objections.'

CHAP. XII.

HOW MRS BULL'S ATTENDANTS WERE PREPARED ON THIS SUBJECT.

Margaret could scarcely expect any other answer from her brother; he might, indeed, have talked to his wife, and it would have become him to have done so very loudly; but the settling matters of that kind, was left entirely to her and Sir Thomas. This circumstance Peg knew, and accordingly wrote to Mrs Bull, Sir Thomas, and all her own clerks in the office, to each in the style which was proper for her to make use of; and as all the originals are in our hands, not to interrupt the course of our narration, we intend to defer the publication of them, with that of many other original papers, to the conclusion of this great work.

Notwithstanding that Peg had taken all this trouble, many people were of opinion that the affair would never be heard of in the counting-room, so much were they used to see Peg's affairs overlooked; but they were mistaken. Gilbert[71] told Mrs Bull the first or second time he saw her, what a suit he was to present from her sister, and two or three of Peg's boys were determined that it should not go without a hearing. Mean time, the nurse and Hubble-bubble were not idle.[72] The scheme which they thought to have frustrated was taking place very fast. The boy George and his companions were laughing at them as usual, and the young men who had been sent out to watch Lewis Baboon's motions, past their time merrily in the fields, playing at cricket, pitch-bar, and foot-ball, from morning to night, eat their victuals with a good appetite, and slept as sound in a barn, as ever they had done in the best bed in John's house: all which, the nurse would not have believed, if you had sworn it to her on all the four evangelists. In short, there was no appearance of their tiring, and they would have held out through mere spite, if they had been tired, when they found that there was any intention to vex them.

All this was sore enough upon the nurse, without being obliged to see her predictions equally falsified, by having the same thing tried in sister Peg's house. This she could by no means think of with any patience, and she determined to do all she could with Mrs Bull to prevent it. For this purpose, Hubble-bubble and she took their opportunity to talk to many of Mrs Bull's attendants. They put them in mind of all the perquisites, presents and vails, which had been so kindly thrown in their way; observed of what consequence the present affair was to them, and that if they suffered their friends to be baffled, and discredited, they must not expect to be served so, in time coming. 'You may soon get other people in our places', said they, 'who will be willing to court you for the sake of your mistress; but can you go as familiarly to a new comer, to ask for a bit of victuals, or a glass of liquor between meals?' By this and such like talk, they contrived to secure the people who had Mrs Bull's ear. And though they were sure of herself at last, yet matters would go much more smoothly, if they could get any of sister Peg's own clerks to give up the affair, as if she was not very much bent upon it herself.

Historians agree, that they tampered with many people for this purpose; but it is well known that not a soul of them would listen to proposals of that kind, till they came to Bumbo, whom they would have tried sooner, if they had not thought themselves sure of him, and at the same time known what degree of credit he was likely to bring them. They had sometimes let him loose upon Mrs Bull before, to very little purpose;[73] although for discourse he was always ready, and had stuff in his head, which might be turned into jocular sayings, serious sentences, pathetic declamations, angry ebullitions, or plantive ditties, with equal propriety. He made the same thing pass in all these shapes, but the hearers did not know either when to laugh or cry, unless he gave them a signal, by a slap in the chops, a remarkable roar, or a doleful whine, by means of which it was dangerous to sit near him; and whether you was near him or no, the changes of his voice produced an odd sort of mounting and dipping, like the heaving of waves, and had the same effect in raising a violent inclination to vomit. They say, that he had often turned Mrs Bull's stomach, and that she always took cordials when she expected a visit from him. This being the case, he was to be employed with caution; but he had still one quality, from which they expected some good, and that was his precise and accurate method of dividing mankind into Thomists and Geoffrites;[74] in the last of which classes, he commonly put his mother Peg.

A Geoffrite originally meant any person who was for restoring Squire Geoffrey to the management of John Bull's business, and a Thomist the opposite.[75] What this gentlemen meant by these appellations nobody could find out, for he sometimes bestowed them indifferently on Sir Thomas's best friends; and what is more surprizing still, on people who never thought of Sir Thomas nor Squire Geoffrey in all their lives; as well as some others, who never thought of anything at all, but how to fill their own bellies and their pockets. He himself, it was said, was a Thomist of this kind; but whilst he did nothing himself, but swallow the warm pottage he had got from John Bull's nurse, he wanted to persuade you, that other people's heads were constantly taken up about the divine right of attornies to treat their clients as they pleased. A Geoffrite was his favourite topic to speak upon; but whether it was to show his sagacity in finding out what escaped other people, or merely because he had never seen any body paid for finding out Thomists, it is certain, that for one Thomist, he would point you out a dozen of Geoffrites; and you would be surprized, how the devil Sir Thomas got into the management of John Bull's or sister Peg's business at all, as Bumbo certainly was not in the way to help him to it.

With all these considerations pro and con, the nurse was extremely desirous to see him; and as fortune would have it, he was no less anxious to see her. He wanted at this very time a special reward for all his services, no less than to be appointed major-domo[76] in Peg's own house: this was a sort of a man house-keeper, and was commonly a grave elderly person who kept the keys of Peg's pantry, and entertained as he thought proper any of the tenants, who had affairs about the house. The last major-domo[77] was lately dead; and as John Bull's nurse took the charge of all pantries and nurseries far and near, and would let nobody meddle with them, but who was of her own chusing, it was not doubted at this time, that her favourite Bumbo would be the man. But in order to secure it the more, he furnished himself with a list of some dozen of Geoffrites, picked up nobody knows how, and containing some of those who were likely to oppose himself, in getting the major-domo-ship in Peg's family. With this provision he went down stairs, and so across the court to John Bull's house.

CHAP. XIII.

HOW BUMBO *DISCOURSED WITH* JOHN BULL'S *NURSE, AND FOUND HER NOT SO GREAT A FOOL AS HE THOUGHT HER.*

Bumbo, without staying to speak with any body, went straight to the nurse's closet, where he found her very melancholy, lamenting her connection with such a fool as Hubble-bubble, and not much conforted with the thought of having nobody now to trust to but Bumbo. However, as the saying is, a drowning man will catch at a straw; whenever he appeared, she got up and embraced him. Which he understanding to be as much as to say, My dear major-domo, I am glad to see you, was going to thank her, when she broke out into a perfect rage against sister Peg and her family.

'What', says she, 'is the meaning of this impertinent saucy letter, you have sent from your house to Mr Bull? have I not enough to do with his own humours and his freaks, without your refreshing his memory, and pretending to copy after him like the ass in Aesop?[78] Set you up, indeed! we should bring our matters to a fine pass, if we minded all your letters and remonstrances.'

'I hope your ladyship', says Bumbo, 'does not imagine that I had any hand in writing that letter, or would put any thing in Peg's head, which I knew to be so disagreeable to your ladyship; indeed, I could not shew myself any where, without the hazard of being absolutely worried by the people who were for writing that insolent letter.'

'What shall we do then?' says the nurse; 'if that vixen is so much bent upon this whim, Mrs Bull cannot possibly refuse her husband's own sister, what the world will call so poor a favour; it would look like mere jealousy and spleen, and might breed heart-burnings between the two families.'

Here Mr Bumbo, perceiving the good woman's extreme distress, thought how he best might comfort her, and thereby turn the discourse to the affair of his own major-domo-ship. 'My dear madam', says he, 'don't be uneasy; this letter was written by a parcel of Geoffrites, of whom I have a list in my pocket; the few Thomists that are in that house, would sooner be hanged than do any thing so disagreeable to your ladyship.'

'Yours are right Thomists', says the nurse; 'ours here are more troublesome about those matters, than any body; but assure me', says she, 'that this letter is a forgery, and I shall love you as long as I breathe.'

'A mere forgery upon my salvation', says Bumbo.

'Well said', says she, 'what comfort you give me! Let us away to Mrs Bull, and have those forgers tried to the utmost.'

'Before your ladyship goes', says Bumbo, 'I have a little affair to mention: your ladyship knows, that the major-domo is dead, may not I presume to hope, that your ladyship will do me a good office with Sir Thomas on this occasion?'

'Assure yourself that you shall be major-domo', says the nurse; 'but you must not go, till Mrs Bull has heard your evidence about the forgery.'

'Upon my honour and reputation', says Bumbo, 'there is no occasion; the forgery will appear quite plain, every word of it forged, as I declare to you; but that unnatural woman was persuaded to desire me to second her application, and your ladyship knows, that even a major-domo leads but a dog's life, if the mistress and every body be against him. There is Small-Trash, the Laird of Lick-pelf's brother,[79] will give his oath about the forgery; and that is the same thing as if I did it myself, for every body knows that we always swear the same things.'

'I don't understand your scruples now', says the nurse; 'would any woman desire you to second a forged application? Besides nobody ever heard of Small-Trash; and we cannot be answerable for trusting his evidence. Stay, stay, my dear major-domo, and give us your own proper evidence in this important point of forgery.'

'I pray', says Bumbo, 'that your ladyship would consider my straits; I dare not say a word about Geoffrites; every body will roar, and say, they knew what was a coming; nor dare I speak my mind about Peg;[80] I beg that your ladyship would not expose me like a bawd on the pillory, to be pelted, battered, and splashed with rotten eggs, chewed apples, and street dirt, for the faithful counsel which I give in your private ear. I will do twice as much for you in another way.'

'Well, well', says the nurse, 'I see the matter is hard, Gilbert and James[81] will carry all before them. I shall neither meddle nor make; Sir Thomas will be imposed upon about the major-domo-ship. There are many people looking for the place, and let me tell you it is an office of great consequence. You are young, Mr Bumbo; and they say, you are hot when my back is turned, and you do not understand much of the larder or the pantry, and you huff the poor tenants when they come about the kitchen, and that Margaret herself has not that confidence in you, which the mistress of a family should have in a person, who has such a trust about her house. In short, I have had many disputes on your account, and now I am an old woman, and don't meddle much. There is little appearance of my being able to obtain this favour for you; but you may talk to Sir Thomas about it yourself. I am, indeed, very much out of order; old age has many infirmities; a very severe cough I have, and am troubled with wind; indeed, I have not eat an ounce of victuals for these three days.'

It is impossible to describe what passed in Bumbo's countenance during this harangue. It changed from suspence to embarrassment, from embarrassment to confusion, from confusion to absolute despair; and there it settled, when the nurse concluded her speech and was just a going. 'Well', says he, with a faultering voice, 'I have got many enemies on your account and Sir Thomas's; here they are, pulling the list out of his pocket, sworn Geoffrites, as I hope to be saved.'[82]

'That will not do, Mr Bumbo', says the nurse; 'we do not

care a rush for your Geoffrites or your Thomists either. They do well enough in their time, but when one is about serious business, I hate trifling. If John Bull and his sister take the defence of their houses upon themselves, we may all go packing. What influence can any body have in a family, where he has little or nothing to give away? I have been all my life contriving things for Sir Thomas and myself, to take to ourselves, or to give away, and now you would have us part with one of the best things we have. I have found, Mr Bumbo, that a person's influence in any family, depends on the number of good things he has to give; you must have caps, ribbons and petticoats for the maids, sugar-plumbs for the children, and luncheons for the clerks, and be able to help a footman now and then out of livery, otherwise they will not give an old song for you; and Sir Thomas has found plenty about John's house, otherwise Mrs Bull and he would not be so good friends[88] as they are. People must have their vails and their perquisites. Many a time has Sir Thomas obliged his friend with a game-keeper's place or so; and consider with yourself, that if John continues to do any part of that business himself, what numbers, not only of game-keepers, foresters and whippers-in, but even weavers, taylors, smiths, accountants, bakers, tanners, and shoe-makers, will forget the way to Sir Thomas's closet, and never think more of Hubble-bubble, or your humble servant. And then the management of Rousterdivel's affairs when he was brought over, was an excellent thing; trust me, many a pretty fortune has been got by Rousterdivel. But it is all over, Mr Bumbo, all over; and now a person who comes to ask for a major-domo-ship, thinks he may do what he pleases.'

'Much honoured madam', says Bumbo, 'I hope you do not consider the scruples of a friend as an absolute refusal. I have always been ready to swear what you please, and if my oath be required to this forgery, I am ready to give it.'

'That was spoken like a major-domo', says the nurse; 'let us away to Hubble-bubble, and settle the tenour of your evidence.'

CHAP. XIV.

SHOWING HOW IT WAS THE FASHION TO HARANGUE MRS BULL.

Altho' Mrs Bull, in all matters of consequence, generally took her resolution before she came into the office, yet it was the fashion to talk to her, as if she was undetermined to the last; and she herself humoured people in this whim, by listening to them, as if she was drinking in instruction at both her ears, from every word they said. This same had its consequences, for she got the habit of doing nothing, unless some body spoke to her more or less, and then if she was never so much determined upon a point, she was often out of countenance, when all the talk and the noise was on the other side.

This circumstance made Jowler so precious a fellow, that Hubble-bubble himself, at the time he had most to say with Mrs Bull, would have given a piece of his ear to have had Jowler hold his tongue; which he, however, would never do, till he saw time and place convenient. Then do historians say, that they have seen him as silent as a lamb, or making his noise on t'other side of the same question.

However this be, you may believe that this affair of sister Peg's was not to pass without talking enough. Mrs Bull was no sooner seated, than there were people enow ready to advise her; she was told to put off the matter to another time, that it was an affair of great consequence, and that Peg appeared to be in too great a hurry. Which was scarcely said, when she was told, that her ladyship was no stranger to such subjects, that she had heard enough of it lately from her own husband, and given her opinion; that the people who spoke of Margaret's hurry, were certainly in jest, and meant to ridicule the poor woman for her long patience and forbearance.

In short, some people said, that they did not think it was safe to trust sister Peg with any arms at all. They bid Mrs Bull recollect, whether she had not heard, that Peg had been in the practice of biting and scratching her brother, when they were both in the nursery; and asked, what security John now had, that she might not beat him out of his own house, or otherwise use him as she thought proper.

Mrs Bull herself was ashamed of this argument; for a woman, whatever she may think, cannot bear to hear her husband meanly spoke of. But she was soon relieved of this distress, by a person who set forth John's manhood to some purpose; and in short, gave his opinion, that to be afraid of so inferior a force was mean and dastardly, to express any jealousy of Margaret's dispositions was injurious and abominable, as they had every reason to believe, that she was well satisfied with her brother, and only meant to tread in his steps, in a matter which would be so honourable for both.

One fellow[84] came running from the pantry, with a bib and an apron, and quoted the nurse's dream; he said, that although John Bull had banished the weavers, it was no reason why his sister Peg should do the like; that she had more need to have a piece of cloth sent her to make coats for her children, than authority for any such pernicious scheme; and that if she and her whole house were at the door, he would not grant so ruinous a favour; that he remembered to have heard the condition that both houses were in, when every body thought himself qualified to fight, that there was then neither wheel nor loom within the door, and nobody wrought any at all; and he asked Mrs Bull, whether she would have those times revived?

To this it was said, that every body might have heard of times, when people wrought very little, but that they always wrought more or less; and that if there was less work done formerly than now, it was because fewer people were bred to business, and because there was not so ready a market for fine cloaths or other niceties, by which tradesmen get their livelihood; but that now when every body is bred to business, and a tradesman's work is well paid for, it was absurd to say, they would grow idle, merely because they could keep their own, and were put in a condition not to be robbed and plundered.

This did not hinder others from talking on without end. Some of your fine-spun faint-hearted thinking people declared, that they did not think that John Bull or his sister could prosecute this scheme; it was a fine one indeed, they said, but the brother and sister were now too old to think of such projects; a good warm bed, an elbow-chair, or a couch, a glass of cordial, or a bit of comfortable dinner, were properer subjects for them to think of, than scrambling over hedges, lying out of nights, and dry blows: That game-keepers might be dangerous within doors, but that John had now no other chance to keep off roguish neighbours: That either his own game-keepers, or those of other people, would lay him in his grave at last: That it became him and his sister who had so many marks of age about them, rather to think of preparing themselves for the other world, than to talk of vapouring any longer in this. In short, there was no end of the impertinencies which were spoken in this strain, all giving Mrs Bull a speedy prospect of widowhood, and turning her thoughts toward Sir Thomas,[85] or some other of your spruce young gallants.

Some said it was lucky that John heard nothing of all this, for he was sometimes as jealous as ten furies, and if he had symptoms of age, he had likewise remains of youth, which would have very ill brooked such insidious attacks on his honour. For our parts we wish that he had heard every word of it, and had given the person who spoke so, a slap in the face; for we do not see what any body has to do putting people in mind of their age, and we are very sure that John will not die the sooner, for doing all he can to keep himself alive; and if he was to die to-morrow, we would rather see him hearty and well while he lives, were it but for an hour, than moping and drooping his head, and in terror not only of what is to come in the other world, but even of every fool who may think to tread upon him in this.

No sooner the rustling, whispering and hubbub which this speech had occasioned was over, then in steps a game-keeper,[86] to tell how much better he could defend the house than any body else. For you must know that the game-keepers were very angry, and treated John Bull as little better than a poacher, for pretending to keep a gun in his own house.

He told Mrs Bull that her husband and his family were mere aukward lubbers, who never could get the strut nor the air of a game keeper to the end of the world; that a man could not fight unless he gave his whole time to it; and that unless a man could fight to purpose, he had better not fight at all.

This speech met with an answer too. It was said, that every body would fight till he ran away; that some people ran away sooner, and others later; that nobody, however, could do it sooner than the game-keepers themselves had done upon occasion;[87] whether their manner of running away was better than any that

John or his sister could attain, this speaker would not pretend to say; but he saw no harm in letting them have a gun in their hands now and then, to use them to it, in order that they might stand as long as possible, if any body came to attack them; and he could see no objection to this, unless it was said, that people were the worse for being used to a firelock, and fought best when they knew nothing of the matter, which from what he had heard of new hired game-keepers might possibly be the case; but that people would probably not urge that argument; and for his part, he had always considered a previous use of arms, as an advantage in times of danger; and therefore, he thought that not only Mr Bull, but his sister too, should have as much of it, as was consistent with their situation.

CHAP. XV.

HOW MRS BULL SAT STILL AND HEARD A GREAT DEAL MORE ON THIS SUBJECT.

We cannot well tell how it happened, that although Mrs Bull was considering only, what answer should be given to sister Peg's letter, yet John's own affairs were brought in head and shoulders, and it seemed as if people were afraid to hurt Peg, except through John's sides.[88] The truth was, that though some people did not like to see the humour spreading, they did not chuse to stop it by objections peculiar to Peg, in which they could have been contradicted; and as the state of disparity to her brother, in which she was put, could by no means be glossed over, they chose to keep away from it as far as possible, and speak only in general terms, Peg's clerks found themselves obliged to do the same thing. One of them told Mrs Bull, that he came there to sollicite a piece of justice for an aged parent, and was surprized to find so many people ready to dissuade her from granting it.

'If there are', says he, 'sufficient objections to the use of arms in a family, discontinue it in your own; if there are not, why disgrace one part of your house, by refusing what all mankind know to be the great distinction between masters and slaves?

'I am surprized, however, to hear so much concerning the absolute inconveniences of this measure. It may be inconvenient for a man to do any thing at all for his own defence; but if it be necessary for his preservation, to what purpose talk of inconveniencies? It is certainly meant by people who speak in this strain, that the method now in question is more inconvenient than that by game-keepers, which is the only other one that I have heard of. If this is their opinion, they should have entered somewhat farther into the question, than at present they appear to have done.

'This family has been for some time in the practice of committing their defence intirely to a certain class of people, whom they call game-keepers. Those are the only persons about the house, supposed to know any thing at all of the use of arms; they are set apart from the rest of the family, and by their manner of life, are made to shake off all connection with them as much as possible; and this, I suppose, that they may be at all times ready to go any where, or do anything that their profession may require, without any regret of their own, or incumbrance from other people.

'They are taught, for the same reason, to obey their leader implicitly, and to know no law but his commands; to all which conditions they bind themselves for life; and in the mean time, do no work either in feed-time or harvest, but are fed at the expence of the family.

'This, I apprehend, to be a very fair description of a game-keeper, as that profession is now maintained. Every body knows that Mr Bull has chosen this expedient with great reluctance. He was always apprehensive, that whoever was master of the only arms in a house, might soon become master of the house itself. The practice, however, stole upon him, and for ought I know he might have gone all lengths in the use of it, if he had not been ashamed of a sudden, to find himself and all his family afraid to look any enemy in the face. He bethought himself of the wretched condition he must be in, either if his game-keepers should turn against him, should desert him, or even be out of the way at an unlucky time. And to fortify himself against those calamities, he has distributed a certain quantity of arms among his children; a certain number are to be named in their turns; to learn the use of those arms, under the direction of a person, to whom all his other affairs are so happily intrusted. The people who receive this instruction live in the family, and mind their business, with the single interruption, which some days of practice, or necessary service may occasion. When they have taken their turn, they leave that station to others, and live as before; with this only difference, that if the house is alarmed, they are readier to act a part, in which they have already had some practice.

'We have heard enough of the impossibility of putting this scheme in execution; but, I think, it is found sufficiently practicable, when we want to have somebody in place of the game-keepers, whom we employ so liberally elsewhere; and therefore, I shall not now say any thing at all upon that point.

'Has it then any inconveniencies which do not attend every other method of self-defence? The expence, the interruption of business, the trouble attending it, do certainly not exceed what is found of the same kind, in maintaining the profession of game-keepers. In point of expence, it is evident we can afford a much more numerous body of men in this way than in any other, if instead of augmenting our game-keepers, we are satisfied with a moderate number in ordinary times, and prepare this resource for ourselves, against any sudden alarm.

'With respect to the interruption of work, it must be allowed, that nobody can possibly work less than a game-keeper. To have so many people idle in succession, or the same number of individuals idle for their whole lives, appears to me precisely the same thing, with this only difference, that a game-keeper is idle, whether there be occasion to employ him in his profession or no, the other is not.

'As for the trouble, I do not know any body who can have cause to complain of it, except Mr Bull and his sister; and when they are tired, they will probably let it alone, without troubling your ladyship for any orders about the matter.

'But I find people of very solemn authority, who tell us that it is dangerous to trust the youth of a family with arms. That besides quarrelling among themselves, they will fly in the face of every body else. That they may even drag your ladyship off that couch where you sit, and kick us your clerks down stairs. I should be glad to know from whom it is you are to fear these outrages; or if any body in reality was to offer them, to whom would you apply for protection, but to those who call you their lawful superior and their parent. It is strange, that a parent should be supposed to have no hold in the affections of her own children, or that they who stand first in point of esteem and respect in the family, should be in danger of being maltreated by those with whom they are so nearly connected. For my part, if the children of this family improve in their courage, their vigour, and their spirit, I expect to improve with them, and should be ashamed to own, that I fear losing, in that case, the respect and affection, with which I am now received among my companions.

'At any rate it seems it is owned, that we may quarrel among ourselves; and pray who is it we would have to be worsted, in case of such a quarrel? Can we foresee who will be in the right, that we may arm them, and nobody else? It seems, we are sure, the game-keeper, at least, will be always in the right, since we are for keeping him perpetually armed, and for rendering all the rest as tame and helpless as possible, that he may have the less trouble, or find them ready subdued to his hand. Or do those who alarm us with the fear of domestic quarrels, pretend that the game-keeper will never quarrel with any body? I would gladly avoid this subject, but the question is forced upon us. I honour the profession of which I speak, and would often in my life have gladly embraced it.[89] But when I was describing it to you, I thought that I was pointing out the most dangerous quarter, into which the spirit of domestic faction can come.[90] Here is an order of men, who are always in readiness to act, whose leader is always prepared; in possession at all times of great power, and at all times desirous of more. Other factions may lurk underground in the seed, or spring into view to be crushed as they appear. But this is at all times a full grown plant.[91] There needs no giant to tear it from the roots, nor is there any great address required, with the help of this weapon, to confound and destroy all the civil and domestic institutions of men.

'I speak not with a view to excite groundless jealousies; I speak in behalf of an institution, which is now compleated in one part of the family, and which, if carried to the other, must prove our best security against ill-designing men, from within, or from without,[92] in either house. If it be an advantage where it is already established, I hope that your ladyship will not refuse to share it with an only sister, who would be glad to employ all her force in your service, and now only claims her privilege as a piece of justice, from a person to whom she has intrusted the management of her affairs.'

CHAP. XVI.

HOW BUMBO GAVE HIS EVIDENCE.

We are far from commending the practice of certain historians,[93] who pretend to give the compleat speeches which were spoken many ages before, by leaders of armies, members of councils, and orators in popular assemblies; we maintain that nobody can do this, except the devil, or some person to whom the speaker himself gave a copy of his harangue in writing. This not being our case, we content ourselves with giving a few broken hints, such as we have been able to collect from the best authorities, in order to give our reader some notion of the substance of what was said to Mrs Bull upon this great occasion. With respect to the contents of this chapter, indeed, we are singularly happy, in having met with the memoirs of Suck-Fist, a very learned man of that age,[94] who used to feed the game-keeper's pointer, and being present with Mrs Bull on this occasion, has transmitted to posterity the particulars of Bumbo's appearance.

By him we are informed, that Bumbo, after all, was not put to his oath; that the terrors of a formal oath approaching, he so explained what he had said about the forgery, that it was not thought expedient to put him to it in public; and the nurse thought it was better to hazard a speech from him at large, which if the lady's bowels could bear to an end, would at least show the world, that there was one of Peg's own people against granting her request.

Bumbo therefore appeared with this view, as no better could be made of it. Suck-Fist relates, that he began with declaring the instructions he had got from Margaret, to second her application. He said, that for his part it was his opinion, that nothing could be more reasonable than the proposal she made; that if John Bull had arms in his house, or sent his children to the fencing-school for a month or two, there was no reason why Margaret should be hindered from doing the same thing; and that there was nothing more desireable than to have every distinction between the two families abolished.

Were not Suck-Fist a writer of good authority, both in point of judgment and veracity, we should be apt to question the following particulars of his narration; they are so repugnant to what went before, and so totally void of sense or coherence, that not only we, but all future historians will hesitate before they transcribe this part of his memoirs into their works. But as fiction is often more probable than truth, we draw a presumption of veracity from the very want of likelihood in the case, and are sure that such things could never have come into any body's head, if they had not been true. To dissuade Mrs Bull from signing the order, which, it seems, was brought her ready written, relating to Peg's people, he tells her, that it was exactly like that she had already given in her own house. He did not pretend, at least in public, that the Geoffrites were many in Peg's house, yet he would not even let Sir Thomas pick and chuse, but said, it was giving arms indiscriminately, to raise turbulent spirits. He commended MacLurchar extremely, and said it was a pity to take him off his loom, except he was to be transported; that giving him arms would spoil his hand as a weaver, and hinder his fighting, in which he had behaved so gloriously, that he did not deserve to be discouraged, much less annihilated, till John had made up matters with Lewis Baboon. He pointed at many bad consequences, that would attend employing MacLurchar, for the defence of the house, such as spoiling a good weaver, and the like; but he insisted, that no distinction should be made between him and any body else, by pushing a line, or any other method that could separate the house into two parts; 'I implore, beseech, and intreat', says he, 'that you would not push any such line across our house; let us all be treated alike, and if there be any of us who are not in danger of being molested, or others who are not fit to carry arms, let us all be refused them together, that nobody's mind may be ruffled, nor any heart-burnings be left, but those which do or may subsist between John Bull himself and his worthy sister Margaret; they have been used to more dust than any can raise between them, and can bear it all.' He advised Mrs Bull to do nothing at all in Peg's house, lest she should forget something; 'when you have shown to us, that you can remember every circumstance at once, then we will apply for your directions, or devise a method of our own; and as Margaret has already born the disgrace of this difference so long, I see no reason why she may not bear it some time longer; her house can never be more open, or more defence-less than it is now, nor her children less qualified to resist thieves; and I see no reason to hurry the supply of defects, to which she is now so well accustomed.' He concluded by telling Mrs Bull, what a dangerous thing it would be to give any orders in Peg's house, when he was told that her ladyship was just going to give some fresh order in her own.

These particulars, posterity will no doubt admit upon the testimony of Suck-Fist; especially as he adds, that if any body shall say, that Bumbo reasoned upon other principles, he is ready to contradict them, by saying it is not true. He subjoins, that Jowler paid him great respect in speaking after him; and we ourselves know, that Small-Trash exclaimed, that he had gained immortal honour.

CHAP. XVII.

HOW MRS BULL SETTLED HER STOMACH.

Mrs Bull, in the course of the foregoing speech, was observed by many people to change colour, and before it was done, hartshorn-drops and smelling-bottles were produced in abun-dance. Every one said, that nobody but Jowler could settle her stomach, for he used to stun her sometimes,[95] so as to take away the sense of every thing else, which has often been observed to have very good effects in trifling illnesses, by drawing off the patient's attention, as the fear of drowning will do in the case of sea sickness, and blisters, caustics, and stimulusses, in the case of other disorders. Jowler accordingly set to work with her: but for want of the big words, with which he used to coax John Bull, and which he avoided now for reasons best known to him-self,[96] he could produce nothing that day, but a maukish sort of stuff, that was little better than the warm water, which people are made to drink after a vomit.

In short, Mrs Bull was up and just going, when one of Peg's clerks begged her not to be rash in dismissing a business, in which the interest, the honour, and the preservation of her husband's family, were so deeply involved; he told her, that he was surprized, to find any objections made to the terms of the order that was laid before her, as they did not pretend to ask any more at that time, than that she should appoint a day to consider that order, and correct it if she thought proper; that if she refused that request, the whole world must say, that she was determined to hear no reason on the subject, and would be left to suspect, that she had as little inclination to the measure in Mr Bull's own house, as in his sister's; for he had scarcely heard one argument, that was not equally strong against it in both. That whether this was the case or no, he never could think the establishment secure, whilst it reached only to one part of the family, nor the union between the two houses compleat, whilst some were treated like step-children or bastards, and others like gentlemen and heirs to the paternal estate.

'It were painful', says he, 'to lay before you at large the iniquity of such a conduct, of which I believe you incapable; but if you are disposed to hear what may be offered on the point in general, I have yet those impressions deeply rooted in my breast, which made me wish for this establishment in your house, as the best security to your fortune, your honour, and your life. Impressions, which make me behold with joy, the steps you have pursued, altho' I am now reduced to the necessity of begging as a favour, in behalf of a parent, what, on the foot of equal treatment, she has a right to demand; and what, if refused, must appear as a stain to her honour, and a mark of disparity which she was not born to endure. But her opposers have saved us the trouble of enlarging on this topic, and wisely made it unnecessary to prove, what is already too plain.

'The arguments are such as would make us believe, that every moment which is bestowed by individuals for the good of the public, is lost to that family for which it is bestowed. They talk of the advantage of private industry, but speak of every practice that connects an individual in his views or affections with the family to which he belongs, as an allurement to idleness and sloth. To act for the family, to defend it in times of peril, is the noblest office to which any individual can aspire; and if he labours within your doors to heap up wealth, without having a soul capable of this office; you may call him, indeed, a gainful property, but will scarcely show him among your children, when they come to appear before those who are judges of men. Who upon such an occasion would point out a sneaking mercenary selfish coward, and call him his child? Yet such is the race which we are desired to propagate, and such is the character which we are cautioned not to corrupt.

'We have heard from many the praise of industry, as if any body were inclined to dispute that praise. We have heard at large, the advantages of wealth, as if wealth and industry were inconsistent with the measure for which we contend. From this source, say they, your store-houses and your granaries are filled: let them tell us then from what source the defence of our stores are to proceed? Will our wealth deter a rapacious enemy? Are the eagles intimidated, when they are told that the doves are fatter than they? No; but our wealth will hire a protector. Who then will defend us against the protector whom we have hired? Is the gripe of a rapacious hireling less to be feared, than that of a rival at the gate? But our wealth, we are told, will enable us to maintain a large and a numerous family. But what is it will render that family worth maintaining, or make the company of those numbers that we hear of desirable? For my part, I never thought it a blessing to be placed in a multitude of base, degenerate, and selfish men. If the people we live with are vile, the more there are of them, just so much the worse.

'I have been surprised, therefore, to hear gentlemen speak of filling a house with men, without ever mentioning the quality of those numbers they mean to assemble; and speak of cloaths and food, as of consequence, whilst the character of him who is to use them is neglected. A little reflection will convince, that the soul of a man is of more value than his possessions, and that the happiness of individuals, as well as that of the families which they compose, depends more on the generosity, justice and fortitude of their spirit, than on the trappings in which they are cloathed, or the quantity of merchandize they sell to their neighbour. They, however, who contend that the present measure is inconsistent with the success of industry and traffic, throw these advantages into a light of greater contempt, than I am disposed to do. We excel our predecessors in the art of procuring wealth;

we excell them in the knowledge of domestick oeconomy; why should we not excell them too in the skill and resolution to defend advantages, which so far exceed what they ever possessed?

'Without we carry this quality along with us, other advantages are of little avail; wealth and affluence are but allurements to rapine; even a disposition to gentleness, humanity and candour, but exposes the more to the assaults of others, and doth not secure the integrity of him who inherits it. If I contend with a knave in behalf of the innocent, and dare not stand the hazard of a contest when brought to extremes, my antagonist knows how to prevail from the first, for I shrink from the countenance of a person who is hardier than I. I am prepared on the slightest trial to betray my friend, my brother, my father, and the honour of my race. I am already formed for a slave, and hold my safety and my life by the tenor of another's will. There is no vice, which may not be grafted on cowardice, as successfully as upon avarice itself, that other stock which we are so willing to cultivate.

'I shall be told that the people of this house are yet far removed from this despicable extreme. I hope they are, and that every assault of injustice would meet with a hardy and resolute opposition in the members of this family; but let us beware of the extremes, to which our maxims and our practices may finally carry us.

'We educate a few only to the use of arms; them, indeed, we endeavour to inspire with courage and a contempt of danger, but we endeavour at the same time, by throwing them into a separate way of life, to weaken their connection with the family, and to stifle the sentiments of filial tenderness and respect, under the load of artificial subordinations, to which they are bound for life. The familiar use of arms may fortify the breast; but more is required to accomplish a faithful and dutiful child, a tender, a generous affection, to that parent, whom he is bound to defend.

'The flower and choice of our young men, croud into the profession of which I speak: for what station is more desireable to a man of spirit, than one in which he can exert the native vigor of his mind, and stand in the light of a protection and defence to his father's house? They place themselves in this station with a glowing and ardent mind, but their continuance in it seldom fails to extinguish or depress those sentiments, and leave no impression but that of a servile dependance on the persons under whose directions they are placed.

'Whilst we thus educate one part of the family, the remainder, we say, are left to cultivate pacific arts; and those arts must be pacific indeed, which render the ability of self-defence unnecessary, by which men are made tools to procure the means of life, and are scarcely put in mind, that they have a right to defend the privileges of men, against all who shall presume to attack them. The former are bred to commit acts of violence, in cold blood, the latter to bear them with a tame and dejected soul. Did we resolve to try what the utmost corruption could do, to debase, to sink and destroy a race of men, a more ingenious contrivance could not be found than this we are disposed to follow.

'It is the business of one man, it seems, to think of nothing but quarrels and violence; to another, it is not even permitted to defend himself. In this hopeful partition of your children, where are you to find the generous, the manly, and the dutiful spirit, equally prepared for times of quiet and of trouble? A spirit, which the suspension even of domestic government will not discompose, but which can, by a well-directed resolution and vigor, restore that order, which it is so well qualified to adorn and maintain.

'If we would have any vestige of such spirit remain among us, let those who have the habits and affections of children, be likewise endowed with the force of men; let those who call you parent be inspired with a resolution to stand by you in all your distresses and difficulties; and whilst they enjoy the privileges and immunities of children, be taught to know that it is their duty to defend them.

'I was always fond of the measure now under consideration, because it aimed at producing those happy effects. You need not be told in what manner it tends to produce them, for your family has already gained strength by pursuing it; and I feel with pleasure, the hopes of a gallant and happy race of men, likely to continue in this house. But let not so wise a measure be partially pursued; let not one part of your race be doomed to baseness and servility, whilst the other is formed to elevation and honour. One rotten member is sometimes found to spread corruption over the whole, and a lurking humour in one corner, to destroy the soundest constitution.

'Your wisest establishments, when confined to a part, may perish for want of that emulation, which, when all are equally engaged, must kindle the ardor and spirits of generous minds. And the implements of slavery may one day be brought from that corner, to which you now deny the privileges of free-men. Into other families we have heard that a master has come, who turned his dwelling into a jail, where nothing is heard but the clank of chains, and the crashing of iron bars. He himself is distinguished by the gloomy depression of his look; the whip, which he holds in his hand, and the instruments of death which are carried before him. But where are the ministers of his cruel purpose to be found? They are purchased with gold in those obscure corners of his neighbourhood, where every man that is born is a slave.

'It has been the practice of other families to condemn a particular race to servile purposes. Their names were never reckoned in the list of the family, their numbers never estimated as any part of their strength. For they were such as by their crimes deserved no better treatment; or by the baseness and servility of their minds, had naturally sunk into this station. But never did the father of a family, by any supercilious neglect or act of violence, throw down the offspring of his own blood, into a state of such deplorable inequality.'

NOTES TO 'SISTER PEG'

J.B.: *The History of John Bull*, by John Arbuthnot,
ed. A. W. Bower and R. A. Erickson (Oxford, 1976)

1 'his sister's lawyer': Union of Crowns, 1603. James VI of Scotland became James I of England.
2 'clerks...who never had any connexion with Margaret, or her hungry loons': James 'left almost all the chief offices in the hands of Elizabeth's ministers, and trusted the conduct of political concerns, both foreign and domestic, to his English subjects'. (Hume, *History*, v, 434–5). 'Loon' is a scotticism which is also found in *John Bull*: '...an old cunning Rogue (or as the *Scots* call it) a *false Loon...*'. (*J.B.*, 6.)
3 'did not harbour vagrants, as they used to do, to...knock out one

another's brains': During the reign of Henry VII many landed proprietors 'dismissed those useless hands which formerly were always at their call in every attempt to subvert the government, or oppose a neighbouring baron' (*History*, v, 427). Here and elsewhere in *Sister Peg* the reader may detect the influence of Swift's allegorical account of Scotland in his *Story of the Injured Lady* (1746):

she is tall and lean, and very ill-shaped; she hath bad Features, and a worse Complexion; she hath a stinking Breath and twenty ill Smells about her besides; which are yet more unsufferable by her natural Sluttishness; for she is always lousy, and never without the Itch. As to her other Qualities, she hath no Reputation either for Virtue, Honesty, Truth, or Manners; and it is no Wonder, considering what her Education hath been. Scolding and Cursing are her common Conversation. To sum up all; she is poor and beggarly, and gets a sorry Maintenance by pilfering whereever she comes. As for this Gentleman. who is now so fond of her, she still beareth him an invincible Hatred; revileth him to his Face, and raileth at him in all Companies. Her House is frequented by a Company of Rogues and Thieves, and Pickpockets, whom she encourageth to rob his Hen-roosts, steal his Corn and Cattle, and do him all manner of Mischief. She hath been known to come at the Head of these Rascals, and beat her Lover until he was sore from Head to Foot, and then force him to pay for the Trouble she was at. Once, attended with a Crew of Raggamuffins, she broke into his House, turned all Things topsy-turvy, and then set it on Fire. At the same Time she told so many Lies among his Servants, that it set them all by the Ears, and his poor Steward was knocked on the Head...*The Prose Writings of Jonathan Swift*, ed. H. Davis (Oxford, 1939–63), IX, 3f.

Hume once chided William Robertson for his

partiality to Dean Swift, whom I can often laugh with, whose style I can even approve, but surely can never admire. It has no harmony, no eloquence, no ornament, and not much correctness, whatever the English may imagine. Were not their literature still in a somewhat barbarous state, that author's place would not be so high among their classics. (*Letters*, II, 194.)

4 'the perpetual contract with Sir Thomas': The Bill of Rights, 1689.

5 'a gentleman in the neighbourhood': Prince William of Orange, subsequently King William III of Great Britain.

6 'Sir Humphrey...the causes which induced John to sollicit that accommodation': Arbuthnot suggested that England was induced to seek a Union of Parliaments ('John's and Peg's agreement') so that Scotland would ratify the Act of Succession, which had been passed by the English parliament in 1701: 'It happened that

John was at that time about making his Will, and entailing his Estate...Now his Sister *Peg's* Name being in the Entail, he could not make a thorough Settlement without her Consent.' (*J.B.*, 54.)

7 'Bull-hall and Thistledown': In Arbuthnot's allegory John Bull's farm is called 'Bullock's-Hatch', and Sister Peg's farm is not given a name.

8 'an agreement was thought upon': Union of Parliaments, 1707.

9 'vails': Tips given by visitors on their departure to the servants of the houses in which they have been guests.

10 'The upper servants...mismanaged their part of the business': By the Act of Union only sixteen Peers of Scotland can sit and vote in the House of Lords. Gilbert Burnet observed that while the Scottish nobility 'suffered a great diminution' as a result of this agreement, 'yet there was a greater majority of the nobility, that concurred in voting for the Union, than in the other States of that Kingdom'. (Quoted in Sir James Fergusson, *The Sixteen Peers of Scotland* (Oxford, 1960), 13.)

11 'what will not a little time do': Hume emphasized the role of time in politics when he wrote that James I could not secure a thorough union of England and Scotland because popular reflection on past calamities had 'kept alive that mutual hatred betwixt the nations...and required time to allay it'. (*History*, v, 435.)

12 'a great turmoil': The Glorious Revolution, 1688–9.

13 For Hume's vivid description of the ancient and modern Highlander in the *Account of Stewart* see note 21 below.

14 'the garret gentry': Highland Chieftains.

15 'kept up John's spirit': According to Arbuthnot, '*John's* Temper depended very much upon the Air; his Spirits rose and fell with the Weather-glass.' But John was cheated by his servants because he was 'a Boon-Companion, loving his Bottle and his Diversions' (*J.B.*, 9). Hume rejected the theory that national character depends upon climate.

16 'the west-common': North America and the West Indies.

17 'Many meetings': After the signing of the Treaty of Aix-la-Chapelle in 1748 French and British Commissioners met in Paris in order to settle the disputed boundaries of Acadia and other matters; but they separated without settling their claims.

18 'none of them knew well what he would be at': When Hume became Under-Secretary of State, Northern Department, he told Trudaine de Montigny that the Seven Years' War might have been prevented by 'the Endeavours of a Person even in my Station'. The account in *Sister Peg* of the origins of the war

should be compared with Hume's account in his letter to Montigny:

It will never be in my purpose, and I believe, still less in my Power, to enter into the Prejudices entertained by the vulgar Part of my Country-men, and to feel an Antipathy against the French Nation: I know them too well to be capable of such a Sentiment. Happily, both Nations are at present seriously disposed to cultivate Peace with each other. May they long continue so: But it is a melancholy Reflection what trivial Matters will often set them a quarrelling, and by that means, spread the Flame from one End of the Globe to the other. The last War, for Instance, proceeded from the most frivolous Causes: It arose not surely from any Spirit of Ambition in you, tho' we imagined so on our side of the Water: It proceeded as little from ambitious Views in us, tho' our success in the War has made that the established Opinion in Europe. It was fomented by some obscure designing Men, contrary to the Intentions of the two Kings, the two Ministries, even the Generality of the two Nations. The Explication of a few Points might have prevented that horrible, destructive, ruinous War; more pernicious to the Victors than to the Vanquished. Perhaps the Endeavours of a Person even in my Station might have had some Effect, and might have prevented so great a mischief. It wou'd be an extreme Pleasure for me to find myself so useful; or even to flatter myself, that I had contributed something to so good an End. (*New Letters*, 235.)

19 'posts': Fort Louisburg, Fort Beauséjour, Fort Duquesne, Fort Frontenac, Fort Ticonderoga, Fort Presquile, Fort le Bouef, etc.

20 'they came to blows': General Braddock's defeat near Fort Duquesne, July 1755.

21 'their barges unhappily met': Admiral Boscawen captured two French ships off the coast of Newfoundland, 10 June 1755.

John Home, in his diary of his last journey with David Hume, reported a 'singular anecdote' told by the latter concerning the beginning of the Seven Years' War:

When a squadron of the English fleet attacked and took two French men of war, the Alcide and the Lys, Louis XV. was so averse to war, that he would have pocketed the insult; and Madame Pompadour said it was better to put up with the affront, than to go to war without any object but the point of honour. It is known, that neither the king, nor the ministers of England, wished for war. The French King abhorred the thought of war! – What then was the cause? Chiefly the fear of the popular clamour, and of the opposition in the Duke of Newcastle's mind. (Home, *Works*, 1, 180–1.)

22 'many changes happen': In his *Account of Stewart* Hume noted this change and offered a comparative assessment of the declining martial spirit of the Highlanders, Lowlanders, and English from the sixteenth to the eighteenth century:

The Great Difference betwixt the State of this Island at present, and what it was a few Centuries ago, is obvious to everyone. At that time, the whole Defence of both Kingdoms was trusted to the People; who, tho' they received no Pay, yet never neglected the Use of Arms; tho' disperst in their own Houses, yet lived under a regular military Subordination to their Superiors and Chieftains; and tho' obliged to labour for their Subsistance, considered, all of them, their civil Occupations as a Drudgery they submited to from mere Necessity, but regarded their military Atchievements as the only Source of Honour and Glory. What Actions of desperate Valour have been performed by such Troops, and what well-disputed Fields they have fought, is known to every one that has the least Acquaintance with the History of this or of any other Nation. And the Behaviour of the present Highlander, who preserves but a small Part of these antient Institutions, may set the Matter still more strongly before use.

The Highlanders are altogether as ignorant of Discipline as the Low-Country Ploughmen, and know as little the Nature of Encampments, Marches, Ranks, Evolutions, Firing, and all the other Parts of military Exercise, which preserve Order in an Army, and render it so formidable. They advance to Battle in a confused Heap, which some People have been pleased to call a Column: They can use no Weapon but the Broad-Sword, which gives not one Wound in ten that is mortal, and obliges each Combatant to occupy double the Ground that would suffice, did he employ the Pushing-Sword or the Bayonet. And they become weaker by their Victories; while they disperse to their Homes, in order to secure the Plunder they have acquired: but still, as long as they retain a devoted Obedience to their Chieftain, who is their Officer, and value themselves upon military Courage above all Endowments, they can never justly be regarded as a contemptible Enemy.

When Men have fallen into a more civilized Life, and have been allowed to addict themselves entirely to the Cultivation of Arts and Manufactures, the Habit of their Mind, still more than that of their Body, soon renders them entirely unfit for the Use of Arms, and gives a different Direction to their Ambition. Every Man is then desirous to excel his Neighbour in Riches or Address, and laughs at the Imputation of Cowardice or Effeminacy. But the barbarous Highlander, living chiefly by Pasturage, has Leisure to cultivate the Ideas of military Honour; and hearing of nought else but the noble Exploits of his Tribe or Clan, and the renowned Heroes of his Lineage, he soon fancies that he himself is born a Hero as well as a Gentleman. The Songs recited at their Festivals, the Fables transmitted from their Ancestors, the continual Strain of their Conversation; all this nourishes their martial Spirit, and renders them, from their Cradle, compleat Soldiers in every thing but the Knowledge of Discipline.

In the antient Civil Wars of *Scotland*, we find that the Highland Families were always of little Weight on either Side, and that the Battles were decided entirely by the *Douglasses, Carrs, Humes,* and the other Low-Country Borderers; who, preserving the same Manners and Institutions with their Countrymen in the Mountains, had acquired a superior Address and Bravery, by their frequent Skirmishes and Battles with the *English*.

We also find, that when all the Highlanders joined to all the Lowlanders, much more numerous and brave than they, invaded *England*, under the legal Authority of their Prince or Sovereign, that Nation were so far from being alarmed at the Storm, that it scarce sufficed to rouse them from their Indolence and Repose. The Militia of the Northern Counties was commonly strong enough to repel the Invaders; and the Inhabitants of *London*, when Battles were fought in *Northumberland*, or the Bishoprick of *Durham* (for our Ancestors seldom advanced farther) heard of these Combats with as great Security, as now they read of the Wars betwixt the *Persians* and the *Indians*.

23 'how this great change was brought about': According to Hume the militia declined during the reigns of Charles II and James II 'partly by the policy of the kings, who had entertained a diffidence of their subjects, partly by that ill-judged law which limited the king's power of mustering and arraying them. In the beginning, however, of Charles's reign, the militia was still deemed formidable.' (*History*, VIII, 314.)

The parliament in 1663 enacted that the King could not array the militia for more than fourteen days a year. Hume considered this law ill-advised: 'The situation of this island, together with its great naval power, has always occasioned other means of security, however requisite, to be much neglected amongst us: and the parliament shewed here a very superfluous jealousy of the King's strictness in discipling the militia. The principles of liberty rather require a contrary jealousy.' (*History*, VII, 383.) Hume believed that it is a defect in a limited monarchy that 'The sword is in the hands of a single person, who will always neglect to discipline the militia, in order to have a pretence for keeping up a standing army.' (*Essays*, I, 491.) While the militia declined, the standing army increased from five thousand at the beginning of Charles II's reign, to thirty thousand at the invasion of Prince William of Orange. (*History*, VIII, 314.)

24 'Some people': For example, John Brown, author of *An Estimate of the Manners and Principles of the Times*.

25 'an old nurse': Sir Robert Walpole.

26 'they must needs keep their game-keepers like lords': Here and elsewhere in *Sister Peg* there are echoes of Swift's treatment of the same theme in *Gulliver's Travels*: The King of Brobdingnag wondered to hear me talk of such chargeable and extensive Wars; that, certainly we must be a quarrelsome People, or live among very

bad Neighbours; and that our Generals must needs be richer than our Kings. He asked, what business we had out of our own Islands, unless upon the Score of Trade or Treaty, or to defend the Coasts with our Fleet. Above all, he was amazed to hear me talk of a mercenary standing Army in the Midst of Peace, and among a free People. He said, if we were governed by our own Consent in the Persons of our Representatives, he could not imagine of whom we were afraid, or against whom we were to fight; and would hear my Opinion, whether a private Man's House might not better be defended by himself, his Children, and Family; than by half a Dozen Rascals picked up at a Venture in the Street, for small Wages, who might get an Hundred Times more by cutting their Throats. *The Prose Writings of Jonathan Swift*, ed. H. Davis (Oxford, 1939–63), xi, 131.

27 'forty or fifty at a time': 'The late King of FRANCE, in time of war, kept in pay above 400,000 men [The inscription on the PALACE-DE-VENDOME says 440,000]' ('Of Refinement in the Arts', *Essays*, iii, 303).

28 'shutting his eyes...marvelously afraid': Elsewhere Hume ridiculed members of the Edinburgh Trained-Bands for being afraid when they fired their guns:

...I remember, when I was a Boy, I had a very contemptible Idea of their Courage. For as they were usually drawn out on Birth Days, and marched up through the main Street, it was very common for any of them, that was bolder than usual, and would give himself Airs before his Wife or Mistress, to fire his Piece, in the Street, without any Authority or Command from his Officers. But I always observed, that they shut their Eyes, before they ventured on this military Exploit; and I, who had at that time been accustomed to fire at Rooks and Magpyes, was very much diverted with their Timorousness. However, I question not, but there are many very honest substantial Tradesmen amongst them, and as long as that is granted, I suppose they will allow any one to make as merry as he pleases with their military Character. (*Account of Stewart*, 15.)

29 'this word *pannic* was grown so familiar with John': Hume wrote about an imagined French invasion in a letter to William Rouet, 6 July 1759: 'They believe already in London that they are 60.000 strong. The Panic is inconceivable. The People in the Country are hurrying up to Town: Those in the Town are hurrying down to the Country: No body thinks of Resistance. Every one believes the French, Popery, & the Pretender to be at their Heels.' (*Letters*, i, 309f.)

30 'some outlandish person, who stiled himself young Mr Geoffrey': Prince Charles Edward Stuart, the Young Pretender. For Hume's low opinion of his character see *Letters*, ii, 274.

31 'one of John's game-keepers': Sir John Cope, Commander-in-Chief in Scotland.

32 'poker': militia. Hence the origin of the name 'Poker Club', founded in 1762 to continue to press for a Scottish militia.

The Edinburgh militia in 1745 consisted of the Trained-Bands (see note 28), the Town Guards, the Edinburgh Regiment, the Volunteers, and the Auxiliaries. Hume wrote that they comprised 'a List of Heroes equal to those of which *Homer* has given us a Catalogue, if not in his *Illiad*, at least in his *Batracho-myomachia*, or Battle of the Frogs and Mice'. The Town Guards were 'rather elderly Men, but pretty well disciplined'; the rest were 'undisciplined *Britons*, which implies just as formidable an Idea as undisciplined *Romans*, or undisciplined *Indians*'. The Edinburgh Regiment was not raised until seven days before the Highland rebels entered the city. 'The oldest enlisted, therefore, were now Veteran Troops of seven days standing: The youngest not less than a Quarter of an Hour. Their Number might amount to about 300. I am told, that their Appearance resembled very much that of *Falstaff's* Tatterdemallion Company, which his Friend supposed he had levied by unloading the Gibbets and pressing the dead Bodies.' (*Account of Stewart*, 14, 16.)

33 'knock on the pate': The Jacobite victory at Prestonpans 21 Sept. 1745, or at Falkirk 17 Jan. 1746. The Rebels entered Carlisle Nov. 1746, and Derby 4 Dec.

34 'the game-keeper': The Duke of Cumberland.

35 'stunning blow in the guts': The Battle of Culloden, 16 April 1746.

36 'so paultry a fellow as MacLurchar': cf. *Account of Stewart*, 11: 'so mean a Foe'.

37 'the ancient conquerors': In the *Account of Stewart* (25) the cowardly English Dragoons are likened to 'the ancient *Grecian* Heroes'.

38 'we shall... place people in that unnatural sister's house': Agents of Argyll and Dundas who spied and informed on the disaffected. Hume's distaste for such agents is evident from his letters. In 1747 Hume sailed from London to Newcastle and remarked: 'Our Ship was dirty: Our Accomodation bad: Our Company Sick: There were four Spies, two Informers, & three Evidences who saild in the same Ship...' (*Letters*, 1, 105.) In 1748 Hume presented Argyll with a copy of his *Essays Moral and Political* and remarked that the Duke was obliged to him because 'I have not incumber'd his Levees, but have left him the free Disposal of all his Favours to Voters, & Cabballers, & Declaimers, & Spies, & such other useful People.' (*Letters*, 1, 113.) Hume held that 'to be a spy, or to be corrupted, is always

infamous under all ministers, and is to be regarded as a shameless prostitution'. (*Essays*, III, 121.)

39 'an obligation to put on his breeches every morning': The Disarming Act, 1747, disarmed the Highlanders and forbade them to wear the traditional tartan dress.

40 'Cracket-Island': Minorca. The French captured it in May 1756.

41 'his own nurse': Philip Yorke (1690–1764), first Earl of Hardwicke; Lord Chancellor from 21 Feb. 1737 until 19 Nov. 1756. In a letter to Montesquieu, Hume praised Lord Hardwicke's Act to abolish the Hereditary Jurisdictions in the Highlands. (*Letters*, I, 134.) Hume's 'two obnoxious Dissertations' on suicide and the immortality of the soul may have been suppressed in 1756 as a result of a threat by Lord Hardwicke. See Mossner, *Life*, 327–30.

42 'the love of money may be forgiven in old age': 'The best excuse that can be made for avarice is, that it generally prevails in old men, or in men of cold tempers, where all the other affections are extinct...' ('Of Avarice', *Essays*, II, 393). Avarice or 'love of money' was Henry VII's 'ruling passion' and it 'naturally led him to encourage commerce, which increased his custom' (*History*, IV, 394). The increase in commerce led to an increase in liberty. See Introduction, note 52.

43 'Hubble-bubble': Thomas Pelham-Holles (1693–1768), Duke of Newcastle; First Lord of the Treasury 1754–6 and 1757–62. 'Newcastle's critics, with their greater intelligence and superior wit, easily underrated him. They laughed at the fuss and bustle, and nicknamed him 'hubble bubble', but they overlooked the patient hours that he devoted to politics.' Newcastle 'was incapable of leading a ministry himself, particularly in times of stress and war. His talents were essentially second-rate. He was prepared to devote his life to trifling details, but he could rarely devise or implement a coherent political strategy. Throughout his career he relied on the strength and advice of abler men. After more than forty years in office he still sought the advice of his great friend and confidant, the Earl of Hardwicke, on how to reply to the Town Clerk of Bristol when the freedom of that city was bestowed on him in 1760. It was this kind of constant demand for help, advice and reassurance that made him appear a fool to many of his contemporaries.' H. T. Dickinson, 'The Duke of Newcastle', in *The Prime Ministers*, I, 78f.

44 'Bawd, whore and rogue': Compare Arbuthnot: 'Jade, Bitch, and Whore were the best Words that *John* gave her' (*J.B.*, 14). A variant of this expression, which is characteristic of Arbuthnot's

allegory (see L. M. Beattie, *John Arbuthnot: Mathematician and Satirist* (Cambridge, Mass., 1935), 39), occurs in Hume's amusing letter to Andrew Stuart upon the publication of the latter's *Letters to Lord Mansfield*:

> I am sorry to tell you, honoured Sir, that David Hume, whom perhaps you look on as your Friend, goes about railing at you in every Company: Son of a Whore and Son of a Bitch are the best Appellations he can afford you. He says, that it is intolerable, that this damned Fellow, who was bred to nothing but drawing of Bonds and Leases, or at best Settlements and Entails, which are the sublime of his former Profession, shoud turn Author, and at once surpass him and all his Brethren...(*Letters*, II, 271.)

45 'Hubble-bubble got out of his way as fast as he could': Newcastle resigned 11 Nov. 1756; Hardwicke resigned eight days later.

46 'a name which has come down to us on the great tide of writers': Jowler is the name of the leader of the pack of dogs that represent 'sharpers' in *The Tatler*, Nos. 59 and 62.

47 'the waterman who was sent': Admiral Byng (1704–57). He was executed in Portsmouth on 14 March 1757. Voltaire satirized this event and the Seven Years' War in *Candide, ou optimisme* (1759): France and England 'are fighting a war over a few acres of snow on the edge of Canada, and they're spending more on that glorious war than the whole of Canada is worth. It's beyond my feeble powers to tell you whether there are more raving lunatics in one country than in another.' When Candide and Martin arrived at Portsmouth they found a large crowd of people

> looking attentively at a rather stout man who was kneeling, blindfolded, on the deck of a naval vessel. There were four soldiers standing opposite him; they each calmly fired three bullets into his head, and the crowd walked away with great satisfaction. 'What was all that?' said Candide. 'And what demon exercises his power everywhere?' He asked who the stout man was who had just been ceremoniously killed. 'An admiral', was the reply. 'And why was that admiral killed?' 'Because he didn't kill enough men. He fought a battle with a French admiral, and it was decided that he wasn't close enough to him.' 'But', said Candide, 'the French admiral was just as far away from the English admiral.' 'That's undeniable', was the answer. 'But in this country it's good to kill an admiral now and then, to encourage the others.' *Candide*, trans. Lowell Blair (New York, 1959).

Hume found *Candide* 'full of Sprightliness & Impiety' (*New Letters*, 53).

48 'he put all his affairs directly into Jowler's hands': Pitt's Administration, 6 Dec. 1756–6 April 1757.

49 'he abused everything that had been done': Those who attack a minister in a free government always exaggerate his 'demerit with regard to the public': 'Unnecessary wars, scandalous treaties, profusion of public treasure, oppressive taxes, every kind of mal-administration is ascribed to him.' ('That Politics may be reduced to a Science', *Essays*, I, 107.)

50 'Sir Thomas's land in the east country': Hanover.

51 'repaired to the coffee-house': In Arbuthnot's allegory John Bull leaves off his trade and turns lawyer: '*John* had con'd over such a Catalogue of hard Words, as were enough to conjure up the Devil; these he used to bubble indifferently in all Companies, especially at Coffee-houses...'. (*J.B.*, 12.)

52 'presently she dreamt': In a long note to section XII of *The Natural History of Religion* Hume delights in showing that even intelligent men such as Xenophon were credulous and held incoherent opinions:

> That great captain and philosopher, the disciple of SOCRATES...gave all the following marks of vulgar, pagan superstition. By SOCRATES's advice, he consulted the oracle of DELPHI, before he would engage in the expedition of CYRUS. Sees a dream the night after the generals were seized; which he pays great regard to, but thinks ambiguous. He and the whole army regard sneezing as a very lucky omen. Has another dream...which his fellow-general, CHIROSPHUS, also pays great regard to. The GREEKS, suffering from a cold north wind, sacrifice to it; and the historian observes, that it immediately abated. XENOPHON consults the sacrifices in secret...He was himself a very skillful augur...XENOPHON mentions an old dream with the interpretation given him, when he first joined CYRUS...*Essays*, II, 351 n.4.

53 'enow': Enough. Hume discussed 'enow' and 'enuff' in an amusing letter to Dr John Clephane; see *Letters*, I, 182f.

54 'I remember you of old': Lord Hardwicke's speech against a militia in the House of Lords, 1756:

> What is the Object of the present War? The Preservation of that Commerce, and of those Colonies. If you turn the Bulk of your common People into Soldiers, what will become of all these? You may indeed stand upon your Guard, with Arms in your Hands; but, in a Course of Years, I fear you will have little in Value left worth guarding; an untrading, unmanufacturing, unimproved, impoverished Country. To this I may apply what *Horace* says of a Man's employing his whole Time and Thought in the Care of his Health; it will be *propter vitam vivendi perdere causas*. (Philip Yorke, *Two Speeches of a Late Lord Chancellor* (London, 1770), 57.) The Latin quotation is actually from Juvenal, *Satire* VIII. 84.

55 'he was a perfect plague to the nurse, who hated a joke': George Townshend (1724–1807), M.P. for Norfolk from 1747 until 12

March 1764. Townshend joined the army in 1743 and served until a dispute with the Duke of Cumberland forced him to resign in 1750. Sir Louis Namier described him as 'burdened with an insuperable urge to ridicule'; he was noted for his caricatures of Cumberland, Lyttleton, Newcastle, and Fox. (Sir Lewis Namier and John Brooke, *The House of Commons 1745–1790*, 3 vols. (London, 1964), II, 549ff.) For examples of Townshend's graphic satire see Herbert M. Atherton, *Political Prints in the Age of Hogarth* (Oxford, 1974). Hume told the Comtesse de Boufflers that Townshend 'passes for a great wit, in our London style. I am not personally acquainted with him; but I am much mistaken, if his wit succeeds at Paris. He will be much surprised at first to find that he is no wit at all; but will discover at last that it is entirely your fault. He passes for a man of worth and honour.' (*Letters*, II, 47.)

56 'Jehu': Furious driver; 2 *Kings*, ix. 20.

57 'some of the worst of them come home...and deal out the victuals': The management of Scottish affairs at this time was in the hands of the Duke of Argyll. In 1748 Hume presented Argyll with a copy of his *Essays Moral and Political*.

His Grace is oblig'd to me, that I have not dedicated them to him, & put him out of Countenance, by the usual Fawning & Flattery of Authors. He is also oblig'd to me, that having once had the Honour of being introducd to him, I have not incumber'd his Levees, but have left him the free Disposal of all his Favours to Voters, Cabballers, & Declaimers, & Spies, & such other useful People. I have a Regard for his Grace, & desire this Trifle may be considerd as a Present, not to the Duke of Argyle, but to Archibald Campbell, who is undoubtedly a Man of Sense & Learning. (*Letters*, I, 113.)

In 1752 Hume asserted that his friends in Glasgow would have succeeded in getting him elected Professor of Logic at Glasgow University 'in spite of the violent and solemn remonstrances of the clergy, if the Duke of Argyle had had courage to give me the least countenance' (*Letters*, I, 280). Hume appears to have been on reasonably good terms with the Duke of Argyll's lieutenant, Lord Milton, until 1757, when Lord Milton rebuked Hume in front of Adam Ferguson, John Home, and Alexander Carlyle. Lord Milton told Hume that it was because the moderate clergy were 'keeping Company with him that such a clamour was rais'd' over John Home's *Douglas*. Hume abruptly left Lord Milton's house and never entered it again. See Carlyle, *Anecdotes*, 167.

58 'never a word of arming his own children': 'The Militia Act which Pitt had long been demanding was introduced...at the beginning of the session but got no further before the Ministry

came to an end.' (J. B. Owen, *The Eighteenth Century 1714–1815* (London, 1974), 85.)

59 'He made up matters again with Rousterdivel...before in this world': Pitt reversed his views on war policy.

For long he had thundered against Hanover, yet his first appearance as chief minister in the House of Commons was to ask for a vote of supply 'for the just and necessary defence and preservation of the Electoral dominions'. Of Newcastle's alliance with Prussia he had earlier declared that he would not have signed it for all the Cabinet offices put together; yet it was now embraced and extended. In the King's speech Frederick the Great became 'my good ally the King of Prussia', and he received a letter from Pitt in which he was gratified to find himself described as 'a Prince who stands the unshaken bulwark of Europe'. Little wonder that there were raised eye-brows and cynical smiles in the House of Commons. (Owen, *Eighteenth Century*, 85.)

60 'one tongue, that used to be loudest of all on the like occasions': Pitt 'felt it necessary to play the game of politics on Newcastle's and Hardwicke's terms. The patriot would disappear, and the politician emerge – reasonable, accomodating, reluctant to offend. These were the bewildering faceabout turns which destroyed his popularity overnight and brought his sincerity under suspicion.' (J. H. Plumb, *Chatham* (London, 1953), 59.)

61 'Jowler kept him perpetually drunk, in order to get his money to spend': Pitt's victories, like Marlborough's in the previous war, created war fever. '*Hocus* and those Rogues kept my Husband, *John Bull*, drunk for five Years together' (*J.B.*, 31).

62 'the game-keeper had taken from him': The Duke of Cumberland had forced Townshend to resign his commission in 1750.

63 'young people like fun better than money': During the reign of James I Great Britain 'was entirely free from the danger and expense of a standing army'.

All the counties of England, in emulation of the capital, were fond of showing a well-ordered and well-appointed militia. It appears that the natural propensity of men towards military shows and exercises will go far, with a little attention in the sovereign, towards exciting and supporting this spirit in any nation. The very boys, at that time, in mimicry of their elders, enlisted themselves voluntarily into companies, elected officers, and practised the discipline, of which the models were every day exposed to their view. (*History*, VI, 118.)

64 'nothing less than a duke or a lord': Emperor.

65 'Lewis had sent a sculler, with some of his game-keepers boys': Admiral Thurot's squadron consisted of three warships and more than twelve-hundred men, including land forces. They descended on Islay 17 Feb. 1760, on Carrickfergus 21 Feb., and

were defeated 28 Feb. by three British warships under the command of Capt. John Elliot. (*Scot's Magazine*, 22 (1760), 98–103.)

66 'Jack...had sown his wild oats, and was grown an orderly conversable fellow': The Moderates now controlled the Church of Scotland.

67 '...*speak with the enemies in the gate*': Psalms, cxxvii, 4–5. Hume sometimes invoked scripture in humorous contexts. For example, in a teasing letter to Isaac Barré upon the latter's fall from office Hume wrote: '*Put not your Trust*, Dear Collonel, *in Princes nor in the Sons of Men: For in them there is no Salvation.*' (*New Letters*, 86.) See also *Account of Stewart*, 25, quoted below, note 87.

68 'drew up a scroll': 'In October 1759 an Ayrshire county meeting petitioned the king for the means of self-defence...' (John R. Western, *The English Militia in the Eighteenth Century*, (London, 1965), 162.)

69 'When John Bull acted from his own temper...his ancient prejudice': Compare Arbuthnot: '*John Bull*, otherwise a good natur'd Man, was very hard-hearted to his Sister *Peg*, chiefly from an Aversion he had conceived in his Infancy' (*J.B.*, 53). 'There was no Man in the World less subject to Rancour than *John Bull*, considering how often his good Nature had been Abus'd; yet I don't know, but he was too apt to harken to tatling People, that carried Tales between him and his Sister *Peg*, on purpose to sow Jealousies, and set them together by the Ears...' (*J.B.*, 56). Hume once asserted in a letter to his brother that 'John Bull's Prejudices are ridiculous; as his Insolence is intolerable' (*Letters*, 1, 121).

70 'bumpers': Admiral Hawke's naval victories, November 1759.

71 'Gilbert': Gilbert Elliot (1722–77), M.P. for Selkirkshire 1753–65; a lord of the Admiralty Nov. 1756–April 1757; June 1757–61. He moved for the bill for a Scottish militia in March 1760.

72 'the nurse and Hubble-bubble were not idle': Hardwicke and Newcastle proceeded to secure votes against the bill. Newcastle said he 'went to work in the old way' (quoted in Western, *English Militia*, 166).

73 'They had sometimes let him loose upon Mrs Bull before, to very little purpose':

Newcastle and Hardwick, equally impressed by Dundas's competence, concerted with him the Scottish legislation for the [1755] session. His chief task was to introduce and carry through the Government bill for continuing indefinitely the expiring Act of 1747, under which sheriffs depute were appointed during pleasure. Dundas himself had originally been opposed to the principle but for some two years past had been convinced of its necessity. But when he ably moved the bill on 20 Feb. 1755 the occasion was not a triumph for him but for Gilbert Elliot, whose brilliant opposition forced the ministry to a compromise. Alarmed by the support gained by 'the Scotch Cabal', the ministry dropped three other controversial bills which Dundas was to have introduced, but expressed 'entire satisfaction' with his conduct. (Namier and Brooke, *Commons*, II, 362.)

74 'his precise and accurate method of dividing mankind into Thomists and Geoffrites': Compare Hume:

> To determine the nature of these [i.e. Whig and Tory] parties is, perhaps, one of the most difficult problems, that can be met with, and is a proof that history may contain questions, as uncertain as any to be found in the most abstract sciences. We have seen the conduct of the two parties, during the course of seventy years, in a vast variety of circumstances, possessed of power, and deprived of it, during peace, and during war: Persons, who profess themselves of one side or other, we meet with every hour, in company, in our pleasures, in our serious occupations: We ourselves are constrained, in a manner, to take party; and living in a country of the highest liberty, every one may openly declare all his sentiments and opinions; Yet are we at a loss to tell the nature, pretensions, and principles of the different factions. (*Essays*, I, 137–8.)

75 'A Geoffrite originally meant...a Thomist the opposite': In 'Of the Parties of Great Britain' Hume provides the following definitions: 'A TORY, therefore, since the *revolution*, may be defined in a few words, to be *a lover of monarchy, though without abandoning liberty; and a partizan of the family of* STUART. As a WHIG may be defined to be *a lover of liberty though without renouncing monarchy; and a friend to the settlement in the* PROTESTANT *line*.' He added that the division of parties in Scotland was into Whigs and Jacobites. (*Essays*, I, 139, 143.)

76 'major-domo in Peg's own house': Lord President of the Court of Session.

77 'The last major-domo': Robert Craigie (1685–1760), Lord President from 1754 until 1760.

78 'pretending to copy after him [Mr Bull] like the ass in Aesop': The fable here alluded to is actually La Fontaine's 'Le lion devenu vieux'. Hume uses the same image in the preface to the *Account of Stewart*, again attributing it to Aesop: The Edinburgh printers were

> so terrified with the Severity of a certain Magistrate...that no printer durst venture to publish it. Poor City! once insulted by the Rebels and now reduced to Subjection, even by those, who ought to protect her. This puts me in mind of a Fable of *Aesop*. An old

Lion, when sick and infirm, lay in his Den, exposed to the Outrages of all the Beasts of the Forest. The Tiger tore him with his Fangs: The Boar gored him with his Tusks: The Bull pierced him with his Horns. Even the Ass kicked the generous and helpless Beast; who now, in his last Agonies, could not forbear lamenting his hard Fate, to be thus trampled upon by so ignoble and base a foe.

79 'Small-Trash, the Laird of Lick-pelf's brother': Charles Hope Weir (1710–90), M.P. for Linlithgowshire, 1743–68; brother of the 2nd Earl of Hopetoun (1704–81). When in 1759 Lord Hopetoun became heir-at-law of the Marquis of Annandale's Scottish estates, Hume renewed his 13-year-old claim for £75 against the estates, but as late as January 1761 the claim was unpaid. See *Letters*, 1, 295f., 337–41.

80 'nor dare I speak my mind about Peg': Alexander Carlyle maintained that it was fear of another Jacobite rebellion, rather than self-interest, which was the motive behind Dundas's speech against a Scottish militia:

> it was said in Party Publications, That this Speech was the price paid for his Being Made President immediately after. But my Belief is, That as Political Principles were Form'd in the School of the Disciples and Followers of Sir R! Walpole, whose ostensible Motive, if not his Governing one, was a Fear of the Family of Stuart, That Dundas sincerely thought, that arming Scotland was Dangerous, Tho' he rested his arg! chiefly on a less unpopular Topick, viz. That a Militia would Ruin our Rising Manufactures. (Carlyle, *Anecdotes*, 204.)

81 'James': James Oswald (1715–69), M.P. for Dysart Burghs 1741–7 and 1754–68; Fife 1747–54; a lord of Trade 1751–59, and lord of the Treasury 1759–63. He seconded Elliot's motion.

82 'as I hope to be saved': This evokes Hocus's (i.e. Marlborough's) speech to persuade John Bull to continue the war: 'There's no Body loves you better than I, nor has taken more pains in your Affairs: As I hop'd to be sav'd I would do any thing to serve you, I would crawl upon all Four to serve you...' (*J.B.*, 36).

83 'otherwise Mrs Bull and he would not be so good friends': In 'Of the Independence of Parliament', Hume argued that the crown must be allowed to influence the House of Commons by offering offices to members: 'We may, therefore, give to this influence what name we please; we may call it by the invidious appellations of *corruption* and *dependence*; but some degree and some kind of it are inseparable from the very nature of the constitution, and necessary to the preservation of our mixed government.' In a footnote Hume added: 'By that *influence of the crown*, which I would justify, I mean only, that arising from the offices and honours which are at the disposal of the crown. As to private

bribery, it may be considered in the same light as the practice of employing spies, which is scarce justifiable in a good minister, and is infamous in a bad one' (*Essays*, I, 120f.). Hume elsewhere affirmed that 'This engine of power may become too forcible, but it cannot altogether be abolished, without the total destruction of monarchy, and even all regular authority.' (*History*, IV, 107.)

84 'One fellow came running from the pantry': Probably Robert Nugent, M.P. for Bristol; a lord of the Treasury Apr. 1754–Dec. 1759; from Jan. 1760 until July 1765 he held 'the lucrative sinecure of joint vice-treasurer of Ireland'. (Namier and Brooke, *Commons*, III, 218f.)

85 'turning her thoughts toward Sir Thomas': Absolute monarchy. In 'Whether the British Government inclines more to Absolute Monarchy, or to a Republic' Hume concluded that 'the power of the crown, by means of its large revenue, is rather upon the encrease'; and that Absolute Monarchy 'is the easiest death, the true *Euthanasia* of the BRITISH constitution'. (*Essays*, I, 126.)

86 'in steps a game-keeper': Probably Lord Barrington, M.P. for Plymouth 1754–78; Secretary at War Oct. 1755–Mar. 1761.

87 'some people ran away sooner... game-keepers themselves had done upon occasion': The Scottish volunteers in 1745 'were believed in particular to have shown up much better than the regulars in the reverse at Falkirk' (Western, *English Militia*, 108). Hume vividly described the events on 16 Sept. 1745, when the King's Dragoons were ordered to retreat before they were within sight of the Jacobite rebels:

They immediately retreated, and began to march in the usual Pace of Cavalry. Orders were repeated, every Furlong, to quicken their Pace; and both Precept and Example concurring, they quickened it so well, that before they reached *Edinburgh*, they had come to a pretty smart Gallop. They passed, in an inexpressible Hurry and Confusion, through the narrow Lanes at *Barefoot's* Parks...They rushed like a Torrent down to *Leith*; where they endeavoured to draw Breath: But some unlucky Boy (I suppose a *Jacobite* in his Heart) calling to them that the Highlanders were approaching, they immediately took to their Heels again, and galloped to *Prestonpans* about six Miles further. Here in a literal Sense, *Timor addidit alas*, their Fear added Wings; I mean to the Rebels. For otherwise, they could not possibly imagine, that these formidable Enemies could be within several Miles of them. But at *Prestonpans* the same Alarm was renewed, *The Philistines be upon thee, Sampson*, they galloped to *Northberwick*; and being now about twenty Miles on the other Side of *Edinburgh*, they thought they might safely dismount from their Horses, and look out for Victuals. Accordingly, like the ancient *Grecian* Heroes, each of them began to kill and dress his

Provisions. *Egit amor dapis atque pugnae*, they were actuated by the Desire of Supper and of Battle. The Sheep and Turkies of *Northberwick* paid for this warlike Disposition. But behold! the Uncertainty of human Happiness; when the Mutton was just ready to be put upon the Table, they heard, or thought they heard, the same Cry of the Highlanders. Their Fear proved stronger than their Hunger; they again got on Horseback, but were informed time enough of the Falseness of the Alarm, to prevent the spoiling of their Meal.

By such Rudiments as these the Dragoons were trained; till at last they became so perfect in their Lesson, that at the Battle of *Preston*, they could practise it of themselves...(*Account of Stewart*, 24–6).

88 'as if people were afraid to hurt Peg, except through John's sides': This aspect of the March debate was highlighted in a report which appeared in an Edinburgh paper for 22 March 1760:

By a private letter from London we are informed, that in a certain house, the debate was very warm upon the subject of extending the militia-laws to Scotland. The question was very fully discussed, and the debate, though unexpected, carried on with great keenness and spirit; the superiority, however, both of argument and eloquence, was (adds the same letter) manifestly on the side of those gentlemen who moved for and supported the bill. We are further informed, and we hear it with pleasure, that the motion for a Scotch militia is honoured by the support of the same friends, and the opposition of the same enemies, with that bill by which a militia was some years ago established in England. This circumstance will at least convince the world, that, whatever may be pretended, the present opposition to a militia for Scotland, proceeds from the rooted dislike of a few men to the establishment itself, not from any objections peculiarly drawn from the state of this part of the united kingdom. And we hope, that although some men are always found to espouse any side of a question, yet the spirit of liberty, and the vigour of the British constitution, will appear on this occasion with that superiority it has always had in every critical conjuncture. England, in which a militia is not only established, but embodied, and employed in actual service, now knows by experience how frivolous and ill-grounded were many of the arguments made use of against it. It appears to have been productive of none of the ill consequences so clearly foreseen, and so strongly insisted on by a certain set of men; industry is not checked, neither are manufactures diminished or destroyed, nor idleness or debauchery become one whit more frequent than they were before. Those who talk without doors [i.e. outside of parliament] against the present bill, find it necessary to reinforce those exploded and threadbare topics, by the addition of a fresh argument, drawn from the general character of bravery ascribed to the Scots, and produce, as a ground of caution at Westminster, what indeed, if true, should strike terror at Versailles. Shall that fierce and warlike people, it has been said (only, we dare say, without doors), proud of the valour of their ancestors, be trusted with arms? To give a militia to Scotland, is to arm Scotland against England. The turbulent disposition of the Scotch, their propensity on every occasion to revolt, makes it necessary to keep them disarmed, and in that respect to treat them like the inhabitants of a conquered province, not the fellow subjects of an united kingdom. (*Scots Magazine*, xxii, 168.)

89 'would often in my life have gladly embraced it': In 1746 Hume considered entering the army (see *New Letters*, 20, 23, 26). His commission as Judge-Advocate of General St Clair's forces is in the Hume MSS. deposited in the Royal Society of Edinburgh. See E. C. Mossner, *The Life of David Hume* (Oxford, 1980), 191f. In a letter of 5 November 1747 to Sir Hew Dalrymple Hume mentions the time '...when I was in the Army...' (*Forum for Modern Language Studies*, vi (1970), 321).

90 'the most dangerous quarter, into which the spirit of domestic faction can come': When there were 'very dangerous Tempests brewing' during the 'Wilkes and Liberty' commotions of 1769, Hume wrote to Strahan: 'Are we sure, that the popular Discontent may not reach the Army, who have a Pretence for Discontents of their own?' 'I wish only the Army may be faithful, and the Militia quiet: Woud to God we had a Scotch Militia at present. This Country is almost unanimous [in its Desire to support Government].' He added that 'it will be happy, if we can escape from [this Frenzy of the People], without falling into a military Government, such as Algiers or Tunis'. (*Letters*, ii, 209–12.)

91 'a full grown plant': Hume also employs horticultural metaphors in 'Of the Rise and Progress of the Arts and Sciences' where the arts and sciences are described as 'noble plants', while law, 'when it has once taken root, is a hardy plant, which will scarcely ever perish' (*Essays*, i, 184f.). In 'Of Parties in General' he writes: 'And what should render the founders of parties more odious is, the difficulty of extirpating these weeds, when once they have taken root in any state. They naturally propagate themselves for centuries...They are, besides, plants which grow most plentifully in the richest soil...' (*Essays*, i, 127f.).

92 'our best security against ill-designing men, from within, or from without': Compare Hume's remark in 'Of the Protestant Succession' that a citizen militia is 'the only method of securing a people fully, both against domestic oppression and foreign conquest'. (*Essays*, i, 476).

93 'the practice of certain historians...a copy of his harangue': Hume himself followed this practice. For example, during the reign of James I the puritan clergy requested the revival of prayer meetings:

> But James sharply replied. *If you aim at a Scottish presbytery, it agrees as well with monarchy as God and the devil. There* Jack *and* Tom *and* Will *and* Dick *shall meet and censure me and my council. Therefore I reiterate my former speech. Le Roi s'avisera. Stay, I pray, for one seven years before you demand; and then, if you find me grow pursie and fat, I may perchance harken unto you. For that government will keep me in breath, and give me work enough.* (*History*, v, 443.)

Hume alluded to this practice when in 1754 he wrote: 'I have got into such a recluse, studious habit, that I believe myself only fit to converse with books, and, however I may pretend to be acquainted with dead kings, shall become quite unsuitable for my friends and contemporaries' (*Letters*, I, 214). He was also fond of invoking the devil. For example, he wrote the Rev. John Douglas that

> from the Commencement of the Reformation till the Revolution, there is not any important Secret in the English History: And, if I could call up the Devil by any powerful Incantation and oblige him to speak Truth, I do not recollect any Questions worth the asking with regard to that Period; Nothing which cannot be known very certainly by means merely human. (*Letters*, II, 229.)

94 'the memoirs of Suck-Fist, a very learned man of that age': Samuel Johnson (1709–84). He wrote the Parliamentary Debates for *The Gentleman's Magazine*, 1741–4. In October 1760 Johnson contributed to *The Gentleman's Magazine* a review of William Tytler's *An Historical and Critical Enquiry into the evidence produced by the Earls of Murray and Morton, against Mary, Queen of Scots: with an examination of the Rev. Dr Robertson's Dissertation and Mr Hume's History, with respect to that evidence.* Hume had nothing but contempt for Tytler who, he believed, had employed 'base Artifices' and had called him a 'Lyar & Rascal'. Hume wrote Lord Elibank: 'I declare him to be a very mangey Cur...And think a sound beating or even a Rope too good for him' (*Letters*, I, 318–21). Johnson, however, praised Tytler for his erudition and courage. See Laurence L. Bongie, 'The Eighteenth-Century Marian Controversy and an Unpublished Letter by David Hume', *Studies in Scottish Literature*, I (1963–4), 236–52. For an excellent account of the personal and literary rivalry between Hume and Johnson

see E. C. Mossner, *The Forgotten Hume* (New York, 1943), chap. 8.

95 'he used to stun her sometimes': Hume, in 1766, commenting on 'a very extraordinary speech of Mr Pit's', wrote that 'men were thrown into such wonder at the lofty and intrepid style of his discourse, that nobody had courage or presence of mind to answer him'. (*Letters*, ii, 18.)

96 'he avoided now for reasons best known to himself': Pitt supported the bill in the April 15 debate, 'but he declared that if it got into Committee he would not be for extending the militia to the Highlands – a curious objection to come from Pitt, who had recently raised his Highland regiments'. (G. F. S. Elliot, *The Border Elliots* (Edinburgh, 1807), 360.) Hume was not favourably disposed towards the policy of raising Highland Regiments for use abroad. As he wrote to Sir Hugh Dalrymple, 5 Nov. 1747: 'It seems, the Government at present intend to raise two Highland Regiments for the States; imitating in this the Roman Policy, who as Tacitus says *Ubi solitudinem fecissent, id pacem vocant*' (*Forum for Modern Language Studies*, vi (1970), 320). The Roman governors 'had carried over to the continent the flower of the British youth, and, having perished in their unsuccessful attempts on the imperial throne, had despoiled the island of those who, in this desperate extremity, were best able to defend it'. (*History*, i, 28.)

BIBLIOGRAPHY

Arbuthnot, John. *The History of John Bull*, ed. A. W. Bower and R. A. Erickson. Oxford, 1976.

The Arniston Memoirs, ed. G. W. T. Omond. Edinburgh, 1887.

Beattie, Lester M. *John Arbuthnot: Mathematician and Satirist.* Cambridge, Mass., 1935.

Bongie, Laurence L. 'The Eighteenth-Century Marian Controversy and an Unpublished Letter by David Hume', *Studies in Scottish Literature*, 1 (1963–4), 236–52.

Brewer, John. *Party Ideology and Popular Politics at the Accession of George III*. Cambridge, 1976.

Brown, John. *An Estimate of the Manners and Principles of the Times.* 2 vols. London, 1758.

Burton, John Hill. *The Life and Correspondence of David Hume.* 2 vols. Edinburgh, 1846.

Carlyle, Alexander. *Anecdotes and Characters of the Times*, ed. J. Kinsley. Oxford, 1973.

Dickinson, H. T., 'The Duke of Newcastle', in H. Van Thal, ed., *The Prime Ministers*, 1. London, 1974.

Elliot, G. F. S. *The Border Elliots*. Edinburgh, 1807.

Ferguson, Adam. *An Essay on the History of Civil Society*, ed. Duncan Forbes. Edinburgh, 1966.

Reflections Previous to the Establishment of a Militia. Edinburgh, 1756.

Fletcher of Saltoun, Andrew. *The Political Works of Andrew Fletcher, Esq.* London, 1732.

Forbes, Duncan. *Hume's Philosophical Politics.* Cambridge, 1976.

'Sceptical Whiggism, Commerce, and Liberty', in A. S. Skinner and T. Wilson, eds., *Essays on Adam Smith*. Oxford, 1976.

Greig, J. Y. T. *David Hume.* London, 1931.

Harrington, James. *The Political Works of James Harrington.* Edited with an introduction by J. G. A. Pocock. Cambridge, 1977.

Hayek, F. A. 'Dr. Bernard Mandeville', *Proceedings of the British Academy*, LII (1966), 125–41.

Home, John. *The Works of John Home, Esq.*, ed. Henry MacKenzie. 3 vols. Edinburgh, 1822.

Hume, David. *Dialogues concerning Natural Religion*, ed. N. Kemp Smith. Indianapolis, 1947.

The History of England, from the Invasion of Julius Caesar to the Revolution in 1688. 8 vols. London, 1822.

The Letters of David Hume, ed. J. Y. T. Greig. 2 vols. Oxford, 1932.

'More Unpublished Letters of David Hume', *Forum for Modern Language Studies*, vi (1970), 315–36.

'New Hume Letters to Lord Elibank, 1748–1776', *Texas Studies in Literature and Language*, iv (1962), 431–60.

New Letters of David Hume, ed. R. Klibansky and E. C. Mossner. Oxford, 1954.

The Philosophical Works of David Hume, ed. T. H. Green and T. H. Grose. 4 vols. London, 1882.

A True Account of the Behaviour and Conduct of Archibald Stewart, Esq.; late Lord Provost of Edinburgh. In a letter to a Friend. London, 1748.

Kettler, David. *The Social and Political Thought of Adam Ferguson*. Ohio, 1965.

Letwin, Shirley Robin. *The Pursuit of Certainty*. Cambridge, 1965.

Mossner, Ernest C. *The Forgotten Hume: Le bon David*. New York, 1943.

'Hume's Epistle to Dr Arbuthnot, 1734: The Biographical Significance', *Huntington Library Quarterly*, vii (1944), 135–53.

The Life of David Hume. Second Edition, Oxford, 1980.

Namier, Sir Lewis and Brooke, John. *The House of Commons 1745–1790*. 3 vols. London, 1964.

Owen, John B. *The Eighteenth Century, 1714–1815*. London, 1974.

Plumb, J. H. *Chatham*. London, 1953.

Pocock, J. G. A. 'Hume and the American Revolution: The Dying Thoughts of a North Briton', in D. F. Norton, N. Capaldi and W. L. Robison, eds. *McGill Hume Studies*. San Diego, 1980.

The Machiavellian Moment. Princeton. 1975.

Ramsay of Ochtertyre, John. *Scotland and Scotsmen in the Eighteenth Century*, ed. A. Allardyce. 2 vols. Edinburgh, 1888.

Raynor, David. 'Hume on Wilkes and Liberty: Two Possible Contributions to *The London Chronicle*', *Eighteenth-Century Studies*, 13 (1980), 365–76.

Skinner, Quentin. *The Foundations of Modern Political Thought*. 2 vols. Cambridge, 1978.

'The Principles and Practice of Opposition: The Case of Bolingbroke versus Walpole', in N. McKendrick, ed., *Historical Per-*

spectives, Studies in English Thought and Society. London, 1974.

Stewart, John B. *The Moral and Political Philosophy of David Hume.* New York, 1963.

Western, John R. *The English Militia in the Eighteenth Century: The Story of a Political Issue, 1660–1802.* London, 1965.

Winch, Donald. *Adam Smith's Politics: An Essay in Historiographic Revision.* Cambridge, 1978.

Yorke, Philip. *Two Speeches of a Late Lord Chancellor.* London, 1770.

Cambridge Studies in the History and Theory of Politics
Editors: Maurice Cowling, G. R. Elton, E. Kedourie,
J. R. Pole and Walter Ullmann

A series in two parts, studies and original texts. The studies are original works on political history and political philosophy while the texts are modern, critical editions of major texts in political thought. The titles include:

TEXTS

Liberty, Equality, Fraternity, by James Fitzjames Stephen, edited with an introduction and notes by R. J. White

Vladimir Akimov on the Dilemmas of Russian Marxism 1895–1903, An English edition of 'A Short History of the Social Democratic Movement in Russia' and 'The Second Congress of the Russian Social Democratic Labour Party', with an introduction and notes by Jonathan Frankel

J. G. Herder on Social and Political Culture, translated, edited and with an introduction by F. M. Barnard

The Limits of State Action, by Wilhelm von Humboldt, edited with an introduction and notes by J. W. Burrow

Kant's Political Writings, edited with an introduction and notes by Hans Reiss; translated by H. B. Nisbet

Karl Marx's Critique of Hegel's 'Philosophy of Right', edited with an introduction and notes by Joseph O'Malley; translated by Annette Jolin and Joseph O'Malley

Lord Salisbury on Politics. A Selection from His Articles in 'The Quarterly Review' 1860–1883, edited by Paul Smith

Francogallia, by François Hotman. Latin text edited by Ralph E. Giesey. English translation by J. H. M. Salmon

The Political Writings of Leibniz, edited and translated by Patrick Riley

Turgot on Progress, Sociology and Economics: A Philosophical Review of the Successive Advances of the Human Mind on Universal History. Reflections on the Formation and Distribution of Wealth, edited, translated and introduced by Ronald L. Meek

Texts concerning the Revolt of the Netherlands, edited with an introduction by E. H. Kossmann and A. F. Mellink

Regicide and Revolution: Speeches at the Trial of Louis XVI, edited with an introduction by Michael Walzer; translated by Marian Rothstein

George Wilhelm Friedrich Hegel: Lectures on the Philosophy of World History: Reason in History, translated from the German edition of Johannes Hoffmeister by H. B. Nisbet and with an introduction by Duncan Forbes

A Machiavellian Treatise by Stephen Gardiner, edited and translated by Peter S. Donaldson

The Political Works of James Harrington, edited by J. G. A. Pocock

Selected Writings of August Cieszkowski, edited and translated with an introductory essay by André Liebich

De Republica Anglorum by Sir Thomas Smith edited by Mary Dewar

STUDIES

1867: Disraeli, Gladstone and Revolution: The Passing of the Second Reform Bill, by Maurice Cowling

The Social and Political Thought of Karl Marx, by Shlomo Avineri

Idealism, Politics and History: Sources of Hegelian Thought, by George Armstrong Kelly

The Impact of Labour 1920–1924: The Beginnings of Modern British Politics, by Maurice Cowling

Alienation: Marx's Conception of Man in Capitalist Society, by Bertell Ollman

The Politics of Reform 1884, by Andrew Jones

Hegel's Theory of the Modern State, by Shlomo Avineri

Jean Bodin and the Rise of Absolutist Theory, by Julian H. Franklin

The Social Problem in the Philosophy of Rousseau, by John Charvet

The Impact of Hitler: British Politics and British Policy 1933–1940 by Maurice Cowling

Social Science and the Ignoble Savage, by Ronald L. Meek

In the Anglo-Arab Labyrinth: The McMahon–Husayn Correspondence and Its Interpretations 1914–1939, by Elie Kedourie

The Liberal Mind 1914–1929, by Michael Bentley

Political Philosophy and Rhetoric: A Study of the Origins of American Party Politics, by John Zvesper

Revolution Principles: The Politics of Party 1689–1720, by J. P. Kenyon

John Locke and the Theory of Sovereignty: Mixed Monarchy and the Right of Resistance in the Political Thought of the English Revolution, by Julian H. Franklin

GLASSBORO STATE COLLEGE